UNDER CURRENTS

CHANNELING OUTRAGE

TO SPARK

PRACTICAL ACTIVISM

UNDER CURRENTS

STEVE DAVIS

WILEY

Published by John Wiley & Sons, Inc., Hoboken, New Jersey.
Published simultaneously in Canada.

For general information on our other products and services or for technical support, please contact our Customer Care Department within the United States at (800) 762-2974, outside the United States at (317) 572-3993 or fax (317) 572-4002.

Wiley publishes in a variety of print and electronic formats and by print-on-demand. Some material included with standard print versions of this book may not be included in e-books or in print-on-demand. If this book refers to media such as a CD or DVD that is not included in the version you purchased, you may download this material at http://booksupport.wiley.com. For more information about Wiley products, visit www.wiley.com.

Library of Congress Cataloging-in-Publication Data

Names: Davis, Steve (Business leader and activist), author.
Title: Undercurrents : channeling outrage to spark practical activism / Steve Davis.
Description: First Edition. | Hoboken : Wiley, 2020. | Includes index.
Identifiers: LCCN 2020025369 (print) | LCCN 2020025370 (ebook) | ISBN 9781119669234 (hardback) | ISBN 9781119669289 (adobe pdf) | ISBN 9781119669258 (epub)
Subjects: LCSH: Social history–21st century. | Social change–History–21st century.
Classification: LCC HN18.3 .D38 2020 (print) | LCC HN18.3 (ebook) | DDC 306.09/05–dc23
LC record available at https://lccn.loc.gov/2020025369
LC ebook record available at https://lccn.loc.gov/2020025370

Cover Design: Wiley
Cover Image: Modern font design © pialhovik /Getty Images

SKY10020775_082720

To the many invisible practical activists around the globe,
working tirelessly every day to improve our world.

And to Bob and Ben,
making this journey possible, and joyful.

Contents

Foreword

As the world continues to grapple with fallout from one of the most disruptive global crises in recent history, never has there been a time for more solidarity, commitment, and action by activists of all kinds across the planet. The COVID-19 pandemic has vividly demonstrated our biological vulnerabilities, but also the complexities of our world, the inequality between our health systems, and the social challenges that arise in the midst of an outbreak. Not surprisingly, outrage has surged around the globe. But if channeled properly, I believe it can be a powerful force to push us toward a better world.

Though it has caused immense suffering, COVID-19 has also demonstrated the extraordinary genius, sacrifice, and compassion that exist within our fellow human beings across the globe. Every day of the crisis I've learned of more ingenious approaches to tackling problems associated with the disease and new forms of social activism to address its many dimensions. Each day I've heard stories of tireless bravery on the part of health workers and others at the frontlines of the pandemic. I've learned of social entrepreneurs developing new tools, students organizing to help each other, community associations rallying to take care of people in their neighborhoods, artists making heartening messages, and companies willing to do "whatever it takes" to help the World Health Organization in its fight against the crisis. Across the planet, activists emerged to do simple, practical, often unheralded acts to change our world for the better.

I can't think of a better moment to have Steve Davis's book, *Undercurrents: Channeling Outrage to Spark Practical Activism*, on my night table. It reminds me that we need to keep channeling our outrage into service and commitment in big ways and in small ones. As we look beyond the pandemic to the many challenges facing our planet in the decade ahead—particularly as we march toward the ambitious commitments of the United Nations' 2030 Sustainable Development Goals—we will need more and more activists to come forward, or be recharged, as they address the inequities across the globe. The five undercurrents set forth in this book are powerful trends that will help us all find ways to engage and serve.

I first met Steve when he was the leader of the amazing global health innovation organization PATH. He'd stepped into global health leadership with new ideas and boundless energy. Coming from a diverse background—as a human rights lawyer, global tech leader, and McKinsey consultant—Steve impressed me with his agile mind, keen insights, enthusiasm for innovation, and determined activism. I later asked him to co-chair the WHO Digital Health Technical Advisory Group, because I knew his recommendations would help to make the WHO a stronger force for digital leadership worldwide. In that role, he would provide useful guidance to all 198 member states in shaping their digital health transformation. This is no small task, given the many complex issues around digital health in different settings—among them, data governance, privacy, interoperability, and ethics in AI research. But I could think of no one better suited to it. That confidence has been borne out again and again. Daily, my colleagues and I witness Steve's behind-the-scenes "practical activism" as he helps us and so many others respond to the pandemic while never losing sight of longer-term opportunities and strategies to use digital tools for advancing the well-being of people around the world. I am thrilled that Steve decided to share some of those thoughts with all of us through writing this book—in the middle of a pandemic, no less!

From my perspective, the world never stops placing enormous obstacles on our path to progress. I have seen many in my life, from my childhood in Ethiopia, to my work as a public health expert confronting the scourge of malaria, to my role in government and my leadership of the WHO during a global pandemic. But I nonetheless remain optimistic about our ability to step around, leap over, and move beyond each hurdle. It is this spirit of optimism that most resonates with me as I read *Undercurrents*. Through these stories of creative, high-impact solutions in global health, education, environment, poverty relief, and gender equality, we see clear themes of courage and hope. But each is presented with an eye toward social change from a practitioner's point of view and a steady dose of pragmatism. That is a powerful combination.

I hope you will find the macrotrends Steve outlines in this book as useful as I do when thinking about our collective future. And I hope you will find your own currents to guide and inspire you. We need each person engaged in our collective work to make a more just, verdant, and healthy world.

Dr. Tedros Adhanom Ghebreyesus
Geneva, Switzerland
May 2020

Introduction

From Outrage to Activism

I am fundamentally an optimist. Whether that comes from nature or nurture, I cannot say. Part of being optimistic is keeping one's head pointed toward the sun, one's feet moving forward. There were many dark moments when my faith in humanity was sorely tested, but I would not and could not give myself up to despair. That way lays defeat and death.
—Nelson Mandela

A REFUGEE CAMP sprawling across a large patch of jungle in Thailand is not the first place most people would expect to enjoy a memorable pickup soccer game. Nor the likeliest wellspring for a life-changing insight. But that is where I embarked on my journey as a practical activist. I wasn't there as a relief worker, just a 22-year-old teacher visiting a friend of a friend who was working for the United Nations. It was January 1980. The Vietnam War had ended only five years before, and thousands of families across Southeast Asia were still reeling from dislocation. They were living in camps and trying to recover, find relatives, and make their way to whatever place would next become home.

The phrase "fish out of water" hardly does justice to how out of place I was, with my backpack, travel guides, and long hair.

The camp sat near the Mekong River. It was filled with Laotians and Cambodians living in tents connected by dusty roads, scattered wells, and temporary feeding halls. The air smelled of burning wood. Almost everyone around me was homeless, grieving, and confused. Most had no idea how long they would live there and no place else to go. I'd arrived as a clueless, but curious, American.

Two friends and I, on break from our teaching fellowships at Tunghai University in Taiwan, had decided to spend our lunar new year holiday traveling around Southeast Asia on a shoestring budget. We did exactly as you might expect from a trio of adventurous young Americans—hung out on the beaches in Malaysia, island-hopped on fishing boats off the Gulf of Thailand, trekked across opium fields in the Golden Triangle, crashed in the bustling hostels of Hong Kong, and ate enormous prawns in the night markets of Singapore. One of my companions had a friend who was working at the United Nations High Commission for Refugees (UNHCR) camp in northeast Thailand, so we'd decided to drop in for an impromptu visit.

Because our host was tending to the camp's children through a makeshift education program, I volunteered to occupy the teenagers with a game of soccer, mostly to make myself feel useful. Despite our lack of a common language, we enjoyed an intense and competitive match, refereeing through hand signals and bits of Lao, Thai, English, French, and Chinese—though I was badly outplayed.

"Where you from?" asked the goalie after we'd been kicking the ball around for a while. He looked to be about 16 and had clearly appointed himself leader of the pack.

"America," I said with some hesitation, given our recent history in the region. While the "killing fields" of Cambodia had faded, the resulting dislocation had affected every village and refugee camp across the region.

"Oh, U.S. We love U.S.!" he replied, grinning. "America's great. We all want to go to America!"

"Where are you from?" I asked.

"Luang Prabang. But I have no home now," he said. "My parents are gone, but I'm okay."

Though he was just a few years younger than me, I wondered how much this teenager could possibly know about the whereabouts of his family, the complexities of world politics, or the future that might befall him. Frankly, I was treating him like a child, a hapless victim, stumbling through my silly grade school questions spoken too loud and too slow. I'll say it plainly: my innocence and arrogance were obvious. Born and raised in small-town Montana, educated at an Ivy League university, I was open to new experiences but wildly naïve about human suffering across the world—not to mention nuanced notions of justice, dignity, and grace. The teenage goalie seemed to understand and, thankfully, cut me off.

"We are survivors," he said. "We'll make it."

Our conversation had quickly veered into territory I was ill-equipped to navigate.

"So, what do you want to do when you grow up?" I asked, awkwardly trying to guide it back toward benign, introductory questions.

"Become a doctor," he answered with great confidence.

"Why a doctor?"

He pointed toward the camp. "Because we must help each other," he said, then looked me directly in the eyes. "You and your friends probably also need doctors, so I can help you too."

This kid moved me, and changed me. Though I'd been at the camp just a short time, I hadn't missed the determination of everyone there trying to create some sense of normalcy in their upended lives. Their optimism floored me. Not a single refugee I met—including the teenager who'd lost his parents—appeared to consider themselves victims. They seemed to be focused only on taking care of one another and finding a dignified path forward.

After the soccer game, I wandered over to the UNHCR processing tent, trying to get my head around the immensity of this place and the complicated issues it presented. Our friend was working with the U.S. State Department, and he'd said I could listen in on an immigration interview between a U.S. official and a refugee applying for resettlement in America. We sat in a small, airless tent—the State Department lawyer, a stout Hmong man applying for asylum, a translator, and me.

"I was a driver for the U.S. team at the embassy," the refugee began, speaking through the translator. At the time, it was helpful for refugees to prove that they'd worked with U.S. forces during the war.

"Where did you drive?" asked the lawyer, checking off boxes on his clipboard.

"I drove officials around Vientiane," the man responded, referring to the capitol of Laos.

"What kind of car?"

"A Ford truck."

"What make?"

"F-150."

"Do you know how to drive a stick shift?" the lawyer continued with an officiousness that struck me as strange, considering the question.

"Of course."

"How many gears did the Ford have—four or five?"

This was a trick question, as that model of pickup had just three gears, and I could see that the refugee was confused. His answer might determine the fate of his entire family, and he knew it. Would they be allowed onto the list for resettlement in the United States? Forced to remain in the camp? Or returned to Laos where they could be in constant danger?

"Four," the man guessed. Immediately, he knew it was wrong. And the interview was over.

I walked out of that tent feeling agitated and confused. My assumptions about America's beneficence, the presumptive roles of aid workers and refugees, and my own blithe detachment from the causes of, or solutions to, this crisis, had all been challenged.

The boy with whom I'd played soccer was not so different from me. In fact, we were just a few years apart in age, both strong-willed and athletic, and I had once considered becoming a doctor too. He clearly considered himself my equal in a very unequal world. And now the Hmong man would be denied a chance to rebuild his life in the United States, simply by dint of a gear-shift question posed by a self-important lawyer. These thoughts swirled in my mind, upending my ideas around "us or them" and "survivors or victims," as it became increasingly clear that the differences between us came down to little more than chance. There was nothing exceptional about me as an American, nothing more than privilege conferred by the luck of circumstance.

Now I wondered about the aid workers. I'd been impressed by their relentless dedication and generosity, even when their task involved making difficult decisions about individual futures. Yet I couldn't ignore the nagging sense that easing people's day-to-day suffering, while a necessary Band-Aid, did not really address their underlying problems. Nor did it provide a sustainable solution. It wouldn't change the political conditions that forced families to flee their countries, nor the economic duress they suffered, nor the government systems that tossed them around like faceless cargo. As we left the camp, I kept asking myself, was there anything a person like me could do to change this?

Back in the States, I would work extensively on refugee-related programs and interview hundreds of applicants for resettlement, learning on the job to recognize the many forces at work in these stiff conversations. Sure, sometimes people lie or shade the truth, but often their memories are tangled by anxiety. Our bureaucratic questionnaires rarely got at the rich complexity of their lives or made room to note the heart-rending sacrifices they'd made and the difficulty of their journeys. Yet even back in that Thai camp, I grasped the basic unfairness. And I sensed a few other things too: our world is filled with outrageous injustices, I was going to commit time and talent to addressing a few of them, and every step of the way would be fraught with difficult decisions.

Forty years later, it's clear that the seeds of my approach to activism took root in that camp. My work has almost always been behind the scenes. I've never been one to storm the castle gates. Except for marching in a few demonstrations in the early days of the AIDS epidemic, I haven't spent much time shouting in the streets. And unlike other, more celebrated activists, I have not designed a game-changing social innovation, discovered a breakthrough scientific formula, started a powerful social movement, or given away hundreds of millions of dollars. Yet, by partnering with many like-minded colleagues around the globe, I've still been lucky to contribute to the improvement of millions of lives through a roll-up-your-sleeves-and-get-things-done form of social activism: practical activism.

There is no simple definition for practical activism. It's an approach to the work of making our world fairer, focused on long-term systemic change. Unlike building homes for the needy or handing out food or medicine on the front lines of a humanitarian crisis, practical activism is often invisible, indirect, and unsexy—aimed at shifting public policies, negotiating partnerships, and innovating to improve government systems. Much of the work is geared toward building networks that develop and introduce new approaches or services, and, more recently, new technologies. But all of these endeavors stem from the same motivation: addressing inequities that cause too much pain and hardship for too many people.

This book is about the powerful forces that will drive practical activism forward over the coming decades. It is offered as a hopeful assessment of the challenges and opportunities that confront us, and the ability of social activists to do even more toward improving our planet and the lives of its people. It isn't a diatribe about all the things that are wrong. Nor does it offer a specific prescription for radical change. I haven't chronicled the biographies of inspiring activists at work—though there are many in these pages. Rather, this book focuses on five large themes powering activism today. I have written it in hopes that those who want to help others might find a vein of inspiration to mine for practical, meaningful solutions to the problems that confront us all.

Though I approach this work as a disciplined, often technical and nuanced, undertaking, every bit of it—from meetings with government officials, to conference calls with funders, to conversations with health providers in the field—is still rooted in sheer outrage. It's about our collective outrage and, really, anger at the enormous inequity and unfairness in this world. It's about how we try to channel that outrage into quieter efforts to find solutions by connecting the dots between governments and people, organizations and communities. And it's about scaling those solutions to get real stuff done, for real people.

Consequently, a central tenet of practical activism is building bridges, usually behind the scenes. It sometimes requires forging alliances between unlikely bedfellows—setting aside preconceptions and refusing to be dissuaded by political differences—in order to reach a common goal. My practical activism has launched me into advocating for foreign aid with staunch "America First" politicians. It has put me in front of Wall Street investors to explain why access to education, healthcare, and a higher standard of living in rural Africa are in their interest. It has led to quiet work on HIV prevention in countries where gay relationships are illegal. For the truly practical activist, opportunities to build bridges surface again and again.

All of us, whatever we do, are working within the context of powerful forces that shape our outcomes, though we may not always be aware of them. So, too, in activism. There are dynamics—economic, political, and cultural—operating beneath the surface of our daily lives that have enormous influence in dictating the world's agenda. This book explores five of those undercurrents and the ways that activists—from the aspiring to the seasoned—can channel them to build a more just and productive planet.

The word *undercurrents* refers to deep and mighty tides invisible to a person navigating on the surface of an ocean. Undercurrents do not always flow in the same direction as the waves on top of the water; indeed, sometimes these underwater channels can pull us backward. But often, they surge forward, propelling the way water drifts, or landscapes form, or social change moves. For the purposes of this book, I am talking about undercurrents that are creating energy and positive momentum to push us forward; macrotrends that will shape the work of activists through this decade and beyond. While these forces have rhythms that are sometimes inconsistent—or possess the potential for negative consequences—each of the undercurrents discussed in this book represents a macrotrend that I believe is vigorous, intractable, and generally positive for our collective pursuit of improving the world we live in.

The five undercurrents are:

1. Pyramid to diamond: Global economies are moving away from the old model of a pyramid, with mainly low-income people and countries at the bottom and a few wealthy ones at the top, toward a fat diamond with vastly more people joining the middle class and living better, realizing powerful new possibilities to link entrepreneurialism with improved well-being.
2. Communities are the customers: Communities are increasingly becoming customers with agency and voice, rather than passive recipients of aid and social change, increasingly playing more of a role in shaping their own futures with community- and human-centered activism.
3. Leveling the playing field: Improving equity—whether based around gender, ethnicity, or sexuality—is radically reshaping the field of social activism.

4. Digital disruption: Data and digital tools will continue to bring valuable new capabilities to our world, revolutionizing everything from health care to education to conservation—even as they present daunting new challenges for activists to navigate.

5. The surprisingly sexy middle: Adapting and scaling innovations for widespread impact, the complex middleware that has often been ignored as one of the less glamorous aspects of social change is becoming more important and, surprisingly, more sexy.

Understanding and exploiting these five undercurrents at work in our world will help practical-minded activists everywhere turn their outrage into action—maybe even optimism.

So why write this book now, when the world seems convulsed with such immense challenges? How can I possibly be hopeful in the face of growing global unrest, alarming patterns of inequality, shockwaves from a global pandemic, and potentially catastrophic climate change? Actually, I have never been more encouraged. Despite daily headlines, which are frightening indeed, a practical activist focuses on the overarching trendlines, most of which are pretty great. Thanks to some amazing innovations and extraordinary commitments from citizens, leaders, governments, and institutions across the globe, this planet is making undeniable progress toward becoming a place where greater numbers of people live longer, healthier, and more productive lives than ever before. In fact, we live within reach of realities that were once unimaginable: a world where abject poverty is rare, few die of preventable diseases, and everyone has a chance to be healthy. Despite some persistent challenges, this is becoming true for more and more communities. Even the COVID-19 global pandemic, while laying bare vulnerabilities in our global health and economic systems and potentially setting us back on many fronts, has demonstrated a renewed spirit of collaboration around solutions, innovations, and strengthened communities. If nothing else, the pandemic has illuminated exactly how the five undercurrents in this book can be harnessed to keep bending the curve of history toward progress.

This book is for a lot of people: anyone who is concerned about inequities in health, economic opportunity, and education, but gets overwhelmed by the scale of these problems. Anyone who would like to work toward bettering lives across the planet but feels paralyzed by cynicism or confused about where to begin. Anyone who is looking for ways to channel their outrage into practical action. Anyone who wants a better world.

I've framed my ideas as a business leader and practitioner to help the interested become educated, the committed become activated, and the engaged become more effective.

Many such people sit before me in the class I teach on social innovation at Stanford University's Graduate School of Business. Others, like my former consulting clients at McKinsey & Company, lead corporations or philanthropic organizations and are trying to figure out how to engage more meaningfully with social issues. And some are people like many of my mom's neighbors in rural Montana—interested, but often underinformed; stymied by doomsday headlines but unaware that if you take a longer view, many trendlines bode well. I am talking to all these potential activists who want to roll up their sleeves and contribute, but don't know where to start.

The class I've taught at Stanford for the past six years is one slice of this audience. Consistently, these smart young adults pepper me with questions about the role of business in society and the effectiveness of our approaches to alleviating poverty. They want to know how to engage with a world that seems broken or, at best, rigged. And they want to see proof of progress.

When I shut my eyes and picture these students, I see three rows. In the first sit young people fired up with idealism. They ask lots of questions and some already have on-the-ground experience inventing environmentally friendly toilets or other products designed to help the planet. Many are not even business majors. But they're ready, intellectually and emotionally, to charge out the door and take on the world.

In the second row are standard business school students. They're attentive, and they work hard. They want to be financially success-ful, but they also want to feel that their lives have meaning and purpose beyond earning gobs of money. They want to know how to achieve both ends, simultaneously.

Then there's the metaphorical back row, full of people who remind me of myself as a young man. Sometimes they're distracted, other times snarky. They seem to bring little passion or commit-ment to this topic, believing that a class on social innovation is "soft," an easy A. Not long ago, one of these students—his name is Michael—approached me after class. He was tall and athletic, with a tidy career path all laid out. Michael was already working as an investment analyst, and he struck me as largely indifferent to what I was teaching. Over the term, he'd lobbed a few questions from the back of the room, most of them suggesting to me that Michael thought social innovation wasn't really *business* and needed much harder metrics to claim success.

I'd formed all kinds of unflattering opinions about this student and what his life post-Stanford would look like. But over the summer, Michael emailed me. He was working for a presidential candidate—someone I'd describe as a centrist—and he was col-laborating on a book about values-based business practices, the importance of business in society and how it could be used to advance social innovation. This blew up all of my preconceptions. It also reminded me that today's young executives view the world very differently from those of previous generations. They appreciate that we need to reengineer our approach to global problems if we are going to sustain ourselves as a species. That group inspires me.

This book is also written for seasoned business leaders like the executives at French insurance giant AXA. Though it is among the oldest and largest corporations in the world, AXA's top managers are determined to reinvent their company for the twenty-first century.

Its board regularly solicits advice from social innovation experts in health, environmental science, digital transformation, and inclusive economics. I leaped at the chance to be part of this advisory team because bringing business into the work of social change is essential. And because helping a corporation think through how to divest from tobacco or coal, invest in disease prevention, and support gender inclusion actually helps their bottom line, ultimately benefiting employees, the communities they serve, and the globe overall.

Beyond corporate titans and the young people who aspire to join them, there are other types of readers I am speaking to very directly: policymakers and donors who influence trends in global development; people who have little money or influence but want to learn how to become more engaged; and citizens like my friend Heather, a former teacher turned stay-at-home mom, who follows politics with great outrage, worries about her children's future, and wants to find a way to stay positive.

My aim is to help turn the frustration of these readers into optimism and, ideally, activism. But I am no Pollyanna. There is real cause for outrage. And the obstacles we face—whether confronting growing race-based disparities, economic inequality, political corruption, or climate change—are enormous. I could write a whole other book on what I consider to be fundamental flaws in the field of global health and development, which were thrown into even starker relief by the COVID-19 pandemic. It is this very outrage that offers the opportunities to spark activism and inspire hope. And there are also signs of important change on the horizon. For the first time in history, two-thirds of all people on this planet have access to infectious disease prevention and newborn care. More people than ever before have reached the middle class, and almost 90 percent of adults can read. Those are incredible shifts, and they portend rapid progress to come.

In *Undercurrents*, I'll zero in on stories from my own life to illustrate important principles for driving change, moments that could be those of any determined global citizen. My journey has not been the stuff of cinematic tragedy or epiphany, yet I've been able to engage deeply in a number of critical social issues as a student, teacher, frontline worker, and leader. Over the 40 years since that soccer game in Thailand, I've worked hard at figuring out how to capitalize on broad social undercurrents to advance larger social-justice goals. By the end of this book, I hope you'll be able to do the same.

These are perilous times, and I understand why anyone might feel discouraged. But the levers for historic change are within our grasp. *Undercurrents* is a blueprint for how to use them and move from outrage to optimism.

Reading the Water

Undercurrents Powering My Journey in Practical Activism

Life is like the sea. Its tides and currents sometimes take a man to distant shores that he never dreamed existed.

—Jocelyn Murray, The English Pirate

I STARTED OUT as an unlikely candidate for global activism: a kid from a rural town of 4,000 people, most of them deeply conservative and proudly isolated from many of the comings and goings of the wider world. I grew up in the ranching community of Dillon, Montana, in a high mountain valley rimmed by stunning peaks running along the Continental Divide. There, the land and the water ruled supreme. So, like many boys in Dillon, by age 13 I had my first job: irrigating our fields of alfalfa and barley. This was in the early 1970s, before industrial-grade sprinklers were widely available, so my Uncle Roy would plow the land, and then we'd walk it, surveying to determine its slope and where water might pool. Next, we'd dig a network of ditches to capture the water streaming from one of the valley's main creeks, and into these ditches I'd drop canvas dividers that worked like temporary dams, diverting the water into still more ditches and pushing it farther into our fields. The trick was getting adequate water to flow over the largest possible area without washing out and drowning our crops.

By high school I'd become quite good at "reading the water," as Uncle Roy used to say, so for several years I was anointed "the Irrigator." Old farmhands sometimes used the title with reverence, but mostly it came with a knowing smirk from family members, who knew this was about the only ranch job I could handle. Still, I loved those long, hot days in the fields, analyzing water. On summer evenings, I used the same skill (less successfully) for fly fishing in the blue ribbon streams of our valley, reading the currents to determine where best to cast my line—some place that would float it into the shallows where the fish fed, but not into an eddy where it could get caught. Later, after I had left our Montana valley and was rowing crew in college, I found myself again attuned to currents and how they could hasten or hinder our quest for speed.

This instinct persisted even when I was away from water. Reading currents—whether natural, social, or economic—and channeling them has shaped my path through life. Luckily, it's also intersected with my work in activism. Among the major undercurrents powering social change during the second half of the twentieth century, four have carried me forward: first, as a young scholar and activist immersed in Chinese history, politics, and culture, just as that country was transforming itself into a world power. Then, as a gay man and human rights lawyer, benefiting from 40 years of stunning progress in consciousness around LGBTQI rights. As the Information Age dawned, I was lucky enough to be tapped to lead Bill Gates's pioneering internet firm Corbis, which leveraged digital tools to overhaul media access to art and photography; and finally, I stepped up to lead the global health and development nonprofit PATH as the world made billion-dollar commitments to achieve the United Nations' Sustainable Development Goals (SDGs) by 2030. These four macrotrends have acted like ocean swells through my life and career, ushering me along, just as a tidal current might push a boat safely to shore.

Though I've traveled far from my Montana roots, I treasure the foundation they provided. Even as a kid, I knew I'd won the parent lottery; my mom and dad generously shared their deep work ethic, intellectual curiosity, and unconditional love with their four children, large extended family, and community. Nevertheless, I'd already swallowed the bitter taste of outrage. I was an overweight, gay kid in a *Brokeback Mountain* town who hadn't yet come out. I often felt isolated and angry, convinced that I was cursed to a life of loneliness and sin. It took several painful years of living in the closet during college at Princeton University before I told my family and friends—with great awkwardness and fear—the truth of who I was. For me, the journey of coming out is never fully over, and I've spent much of my life channeling this early shame into personal, political, and community transformation, as you will see across the pages of this book.

Running parallel to this journey, a second powerful force was similarly shaping my sense of identity. After graduating from college, unsure of what to do with my degree in religious studies, I spent a year teaching in central Taiwan and became enamored of all things Chinese. It was a complicated love since I was intimidated by the language and unnerved by the authoritarian political regime, while mesmerized by the country's complex history and culture. I learned the language, savored its cuisine, found my first boyfriend, and built lifelong bonds in Taiwan and China. Despite my disagreement with some of China's political positions, particularly around human rights, I've been a Sinophile ever since.

These two social forces—the ascendance of China and momentum around gay rights—took root then, during the late 1970s and early 1980s, and became powerful undercurrents that would propel my life and career for four decades. Not that I had the prescience to predict their world-changing power at the time. Rather, I followed those currents because they spoke to my intellectual curiosity, appetite for challenge, and determination to be true to myself. Much of the momentum came from the sheer luck of being in the right place at the right time. But I did begin to recognize that these two movements represented watershed moments in history. These undercurrents also connected me with extraordinary communities of social changemakers who further shaped my work in activism.

By late 1980, I was back home in the United States, expecting to live briefly in a friend's basement apartment in Seattle until I could return to Asia. Then I met Bob, the man I would eventually marry (when we were finally allowed to, decades later). I remember telling him about my experience in the Thai refugee camp, the dignity and determination of the teenage soccer player who'd lost his parents, the humiliation and disappointment of the Hmong man tripped up by a trick question posed by an immigration official. I could barely articulate the dimensions of my outrage and confusion. But Bob sensed them, and he suggested I channel those emotions to work helping other refugees and asylum seekers. So I decided to stay in Seattle and landed a job in refugee resettlement. For the next several years I used whatever skills I possessed, along with a lot of youthful enthusiasm and self-righteous zeal, to help find funding, provide services, and boost community support for Southeast Asian, Cuban, and African newcomers to the Pacific Northwest. It was my first full-time job as an activist. The pay was about $600 per month. I was far from the frontlines and removed from policy discussions in Geneva and Washington, DC. But I was learning the messy nuts and bolts of practical activism—finding homes for families, signing up people for food stamps, processing applications for resettlement, and writing complaint letters about faulty programs and weak regulations. Most of all, this was where

I began learning how to translate my outrage into longer-term practical solutions and help others do the same.

I was still deeply interested in China, however, and a couple years later decided to pursue a master's degree in Chinese studies. Part of that program meant spending the summer of 1983 in China, in one of the first foreign student groups allowed to study there since the Cultural Revolution. We numbered about 40, all of us living together in a funky, old dorm at the edge of the Beijing University campus—a few Americans, a great guy from Japan who became my lifelong friend, a couple of Europeans, and about 20 North Koreans. Vestiges of the Cultural Revolution were still much in evidence, and they touched every part of our lives, including bleak cafeteria meals consisting of rice, cabbage, and eggplant—every single day. Many of us, accustomed to lots more protein, felt like we were starving.

Oddly, being a foreigner afforded me certain freedoms that ordinary Chinese could not enjoy, one of which was access to the few international hotels. Consequently, I regularly hopped the fence with my buddy from Japan, Seido—partly for joyriding on our cool Phoenix bicycles down the grand boulevards, partly to forage for protein. Together, we cruised through old neighborhoods and along mostly carless streets to one of the few tourist hotels in Beijing, heading straight to the bar—more for the peanuts than the beer. They were protein, after all, and we'd stealthily stuff our pockets, later presenting this bounty to our hungry colleagues back at the dorms, where we spread our loot across the beds like kids assessing Halloween candies. While I've never considered myself a rule-breaker, I was, even then, a problem-solver. And I've always enjoyed figuring out creative ways to get stuff done for my team.

After returning to the States, I changed course again: rather than seeking a doctorate in Chinese politics and an academic career, I doubled down on building my toolkit for social justice work and pivoted toward legal studies. An unusual dual-focus program at Columbia University would combine my interests in international human rights and Chinese law, so, with more than a bit of hand-wringing, Bob agreed to sell his construction business and move across the country with me for a new adventure. This was 10 years after the Stonewall demonstrations, and we envisioned ourselves heading toward some sort of gay Mecca where we'd be surrounded by like-minded activist couples while I pursued my degree. At least, that was the plan.

New York, however, turned out to be different than we'd anticipated. Despite the city's reputation for wild liberalism, its gay community in the mid-1980s remained ghettoized. Of the few gay students in my law classes, most were deeply closeted due to fears that being "out" might dash their prospects at the Wall Street firms where they hoped to work. Bob and I, meanwhile, had applied for married student housing. (By then, we'd been together for five years.) When we learned we "didn't qualify," I found myself arguing with the law school dean on my very first day. He was a highly regarded constitutional lawyer but informed me that making the case for a male couple to get into married student housing would be "way too awkward" for the women in the campus housing office. Bob and I were packed off to a tiny room facing an air shaft, where we had to pull out our futon bed each night and roll it up again every morning. This went on for three years. Add in the everyday challenges of being an openly gay couple in the 1980s—when anti-homosexual discrimination in housing, employment, healthcare, and military service were rife—and my sense of injustice was beginning to boil. Then came AIDS.

It is difficult to capture the swirl of terror and outrage I felt as this disease moved from a media story to a force claiming my classmates and acquaintances, one by one, particularly after Bob and I returned to Seattle after graduation. We became caretakers for dying friends, attended funerals of men in the prime of their lives, and lived in abject terror of the virus. I suddenly found myself—a studious kid from a conservative community—at street protests and gay rights parades. Marching channeled my rage, but it left me frustrated.

Protesting was necessary but insufficient to produce the tangible outcomes, like funding for AIDS research or changes to insurance laws, that would improve the well-being of our community.

This was the moment I began to appreciate the important difference between frontline demonstrations and deeper reform. It was also the dawning of my realization of the power in behind-the-scenes practical activism. Let me be clear: I am profoundly grateful that there were, and still are, people driven to speak up loudly for change. Even when strident or off-putting (like the ACT-UP protests at St. Patrick's Cathedral in New York in 1989), public actions garner the attention of media and influencers, which is essential for pushing an issue onto broader public consciousness and, eventually, the agenda of policymakers. Indeed, considering the many harmful policies and the extraordinary affronts to our democratic systems today, I believe much more of this vocal activism is necessary to have any hope of leaving a better world to our children. Every tool matters, from advocacy efforts, to street marches, to effective social media campaigns (beyond merely sharing our outrage by "liking" a headline on Facebook).

But I knew even then that I was more effective as a behind-the-scenes strategist. Shaping policies (on anti-discrimination and pro-marriage laws); building alliances (with straight allies and the business community); designing programs (like Lambert House for gay and lesbian youth in Seattle); donating and raising money (for scores of LGBTQI college scholarships and LGBTQI rights organizations); or working on longer-term systems change—these are the things that charge me up. The work of many activists across multiple platforms and generations laid the building blocks for each of those steps, paving the way for social change. We wouldn't have same-sex marriage across the United States today without winning early legal fights to amend healthcare laws so that AIDS patients could be covered and their partners seen as family. Nor would Bob and I have been able to adopt our son without the underlying work of so many activists who fought to change family law and societal norms.

Thinking back to those years, I can hardly believe the dramatic changes generated by the undercurrents of gay activism and China's ascendance—complete transformations in just a few decades! The notion of legal same-sex marriage was simply inconceivable to me as a young man when I first came out in Taiwan. The idea of China as a global superpower would have been impossible to reconcile with the poverty and isolation I saw in 1983 while traveling on third-class "hard seats" through rural Shandong Province. And to have raised an adopted child from China who grew up the legal son of two dads belies anything I could have dreamed of as a young irrigator in Montana. Yet here we are. Change on a grand scale is possible, and it can happen relatively fast.

The third undercurrent of social evolution that I rode came largely from being in the right place at the right time and willing to leap into the unknown. With my graduate degree in hand, Bob and I returned to Seattle, where I worked in international law and he taught in low-income elementary schools. But after the 1989 Tiananmen Square Massacre dashed the hopes of many for a more democratic China, I pivoted from human rights to focus on another type of rights: intellectual property. Here we were, living in an emerging tech capital just as software was beginning to transform the world, and my law firm was merging with that of Bill Gates, Sr. (father to the Microsoft co-founder). The next thing I knew, I had a front-row seat to the digital revolution.

In 1993, I was recruited to work at Corbis, the groundbreaking startup founded by Bill Gates, the tech pioneer. It sounds old hat now, but Corbis was at the forefront of developing technology through which media companies could access and digitize millions of art and photography images. This meant we were also rethinking copyright law and business models; traveling the world to evangelize for this kind of broad access; and meeting with prominent figures in the worlds of art, photography, and technology. It was a heady and extraordinary opportunity, chock-full of some remarkable achievements and many painful failures. We produced several award-winning products and documentaries using these new technologies, developed cataloguing schemes and rights-management tools, and built alliances between artists, technologists, and businesspeople. After a few years, I was tapped to become the CEO and led Corbis's expansion into a global firm. That time of my life could fill a whole separate book; suffice to say, the Digital Revolution opened my eyes to the power and possibilities in innovation and data. This new undercurrent would influence my activist agenda by making clear that world change would come through the deployment of new technologies, including what we then called the "information superhighway," later known as the internet.

About 15 years ago, these three forces intersected with a fourth undercurrent that would shape the rest of my life and career to date. At the turn of the century—while I was head-down running a pioneering internet company, worrying about Y2K, and wondering if people would ever use credit cards online—in New York City, every member state of the United Nations had endorsed eight Millennial Development Goals (MDGs). These were benchmarks that would measure global efforts to tackle poverty, improve health, and address inequity by 2015. I had no idea this was happening, but my then-boss and friend Bill Gates and his wife, Melinda, were part of it, alongside other philanthropists and political leaders. Under the enlightened leadership of UN Secretary General Kofi Anan, the MDGs would hasten a revolution in the fields of global development and social innovation.

I could not resist this. Such a powerful global movement presented a fertile field to till with the lessons I'd learned through a lifetime of work in leadership and social activism. So, in 2007,

I left Corbis to return to promoting opportunities for impact at the intersection of innovation and social justice, becoming global director of social innovation at McKinsey & Company, where I worked on social sector projects worldwide. I also served on several corporate and nonprofit boards, including at PATH, then known as the Program for Appropriate Technology in Health, a global nonprofit focused on innovations to advance human well-being. I fell in love with PATH's mission, later serving as interim director of its India program, and then its CEO for almost eight years. That fourth undercurrent and my experiences working within it are the primary basis for the ideas in this book.

Leading PATH provided me with a master class in practical activism. I learned a great deal about when to push, where to pull back, and how to get stuff done—a lot of stuff. During my tenure, we raised more than US$2.5 billion for global health innovations and helped to develop hundreds of vaccines, drugs, diagnostics, tools, and digital systems that are reaching hundreds of millions of people and changing human health. In fact, riding this current in global development has deepened my belief in the power of practical activism. Because, frankly, the progress I've seen is astounding. Dare I say, it makes me even more optimistic—even in the wake of crises like COVID-19. Consider:

- In 1979, one child out of eight died before turning five. Today, it's less than one in 20.
- Forty years ago, 30 percent of people on this planet subsisted on less than $2 a day. Today, extreme poverty affects fewer than 10 percent.
- Innovations in treatment for tuberculosis and malaria have saved more than 20 million lives since the start of this century.
- And in most places, HIV infection rates are declining, with a dramatic drop in deaths due to AIDS.

None of these milestones was inevitable. Each resulted from the hard work of people around the globe—research scientists, community health workers, activists, and legislators. Still, the question I am asked more often than any other is how I remain optimistic in the face of so much suffering. The work itself provides my answer. In fact, despite some terrifying headlines, there has never been a time of greater health and prosperity in human history. The past four decades have proven that cooperation between government, business, and the social sector can shrink poverty rates that once looked intractable and eliminate diseases that seemed undefeatable. There is no reason we can't do the same with present-day ills, including climate change, biosecurity threats, and widening economic inequality.

As you will see in the coming pages, most of my time at PATH was spent figuring out better ways to meet the needs of the developing world. But the reasons I've found for optimism abroad exist at home too. For instance, consider the devastating crisis of opioid addiction. This remains a full-scale disaster in the United States, estimated to cost our economy some $400 billion in medical interventions, foster care, and special education over the next 20 years. But slowly, we are beginning to develop procedures for stemming that tide, primarily by treating addiction as a public health problem rather than a moral failing, and getting anti-addiction medication to more people. Still, in Seattle, a city shaped by the likes of Boeing, Microsoft, and Amazon, the clash of extreme affluence and dire need is evident on our streets every single day. At home as abroad, the key to progress is acknowledging a dire reality while remembering that it is fully within our capability to bend the arc of the future toward better ends.

My colleagues and partners at PATH taught me much about channeling outrage into optimism. Every day, they demonstrated the heavy lifting of practical activism, what it takes to jump in, work behind the scenes on complicated issues, and commit to life-changing impact over decades of relentless effort. They also helped me to shape my energy more productively, helping me understand the critical role of compromise in getting stuff done.

Compromise does not mean weakness; if used well, it is almost always a sign of strength. But it's not an easy balance, and often means working with influencers in business or philanthropy whose politics do not align with mine. It has landed me in front of world leaders whose record on human rights is abysmal. It has found me advocating for issues that some would consider counter to my own interests—campaigning for an income tax in my home state of Washington, for instance. Compromise has pushed me toward doing things that were awkward but important, like getting married at a walk-in chapel in a San Jose strip mall so that Bob and I could be part of the early same-sex marriage movement ahead of California's controversial Proposition 8 vote—though a marriage certificate was not important to us personally. Compromise has often forced me to weigh ends against the means of reaching them. In New York City, though Bob and I never got to live in married-student housing, we did influence the university's policies around housing for students to come.

More recently at PATH, we worked with parliamentarians in Uganda who were contemplating laws that could sentence gay people to death. Should their attitudes preclude our engagement with that country around public health? Not if the goal is improving equity and safeguarding human rights. And while PATH endorsed imperatives on inclusivity, we regularly sought common ground with conservative policymakers to push progress on other issues. I am adamant, for example, about women having access to family planning choices, but I am also always willing to sit down with anti–family planning policymakers to see if we can come together on maternal and child-health programs. Similarly, we worked with partners from Uganda, to Myanmar, to Ukraine and other countries where there are clear problems regarding human rights, authoritarianism, or corruption. Because the children who live in those places have as much right to better health as children everywhere.

These kinds of tensions in practical activism have been most pronounced through my lifelong work with China. Following a short talk I gave at the 2011 TED Conference in Long Beach, California—intended to do some myth-busting about China's work in Africa—I was immediately pilloried by both sides: those who felt I was an apologist for China's aggressive engagements across Africa, and those who were angry that I'd criticized China's human rights and environmental record from a TED stage. This moment captured the essence of the challenges around engaging with China as it has become a global superpower. Yes, there is much to condemn and many policies about which to be wary. But there is also so much to gain. China is within reach of eliminating chronic poverty from its population of 1.5 billion people. After fighting some 30 million cases of malaria and facing down more than 30,000 deaths each year through the mid-twentieth century, China is now on the verge of being declared malaria-free by the World Health Organization (WHO). How can we ignore progress like that? What can we learn from a country that has brought more people into the middle class faster than any other in human history? China also has extraordinary assets in science and technology that could advance progress in fighting hunger and disease worldwide. Over the years PATH and its partners have chosen to focus on these opportunities, collaborating with China to access new vaccines and drugs for the developing world; help forge better policies related to digital health systems; and simultaneously navigate the ever-changing political waters that engagement with China inevitably demands.

This practical approach to activism has enabled me to bridge divides that seem insurmountable, or at least logistically improbable. It's sometimes a confusing balancing act, visiting villages in western Myanmar where people barely subsist on daily rations of rice, then jetting off to speak to the .001 percent at Davos. Or talking with sex workers in roadside brothels in Zambia one week, and the next visiting the White House to discuss global development policies; learning about disruptive technologies at a Silicon Valley innovation conference, then sharing basic tips for nutrition with migrants in the urban slums of Dar es Salaam. Practical activism requires this kind of agility. It means building unlikely relationships with unexpected partners and playing different roles, all within the same 24 hours.

Not long ago, I attended a dinner in Kinshasa, capital city of the Democratic Republic of the Congo (DRC). Decimated by 20 years of war and internal conflict, the DRC is one of the poorest nations on the planet and rife with corruption. Of the 186 countries on the United Nations Human Development Index, the DRC ranks nearly last. Three out of four people there live on less than $2 a day. Yet my dinner companions—young doctors and medical researchers—were hopeful, even joyful, about new immunization programs, HIV-prevention tools, and family planning methods that PATH and its partners had helped bring to the country. They were trying to deliver healthcare to 80 million people in a country the size of Western Europe, where roads, electricity, clinics, medicine, and doctors were all in short supply. My tablemates were buzzing about the positive differences they'd already seen in Congo's rural villages and city slums: the improvements coming through innovative health tools and a slowly improving public health system; the way capabilities are expanding with a new generation of well-educated Congolese around the world who have returned to help rebuild their country; and the new opportunities for eliminating old diseases like polio and sleeping sickness. With their nation finally moving toward peace and stability, these health leaders saw themselves at a turning point, and their optimism was contagious.

None of the undercurrents in my life—gay rights, China's ascendance, evolving technology, or the revolution in global development—were things I had forecast; rather, it was more a matter of recognizing what was happening around me and embracing it. My ability to do so was a scaled-up version of my old childhood talent for reading the waters. As an activist, this work needs to happen at two levels, simultaneously.

Many social currents are clearly visible at the surface—for instance, climate change. Preventing and mitigating the impacts of a warmer climate will dictate aspects of health funding and agricultural innovation for decades to come. The need to address climate change is obvious, critical, and—as enshrined in the 17 United Nations' SDGs for 2015 to 2030—already shaping the direction of global development.

Many other acute challenges facing society are also visible on the surface: growing inequality, homelessness, mass incarceration and its devastating effect on communities, pandemics emerging in countries without universal health coverage. The list goes on. Each of these is vital to address, and they appear throughout this book to illustrate its overall thesis.

But our primary focus is undercurrents, the powerful macrotrends that exist beneath the surface. Often, it is the immense size of these undercurrents that blinds us. These forces are so all-encompassing that they form a backdrop to the everyday, such that we may overlook them as individual forces to be harnessed for good. Exactly how does one learn to identify which trends are broad and deep enough to shape the future, then marshal their strength for positive change? We'll discuss that in the coming pages. If my life is any example, you must be curious, able to tolerate risk, willing to trust your gut, and, perhaps most fundamentally, remain optimistic.

Reading the waters in front of us, and focusing on the major forces that will shape the next decades in human development, I believe the following five powerful undercurrents will be pivotal.

My hope is that activists reading this book will use them to make a difference:

1. Pyramid to diamond. Our global economy is changing dramatically. Throughout the twentieth century, the world's economy was depicted as a pyramid, with wealthy countries at the apex and a vast base of the desperately poor. Now, as hundreds of thousands of people move into the middle class every day, that pyramid is morphing into a squat diamond. This means greater capacities for change across much of the developing world, and it will fundamentally alter the premise, approach, and tools we use as changemakers.

2. Communities are the customers. A shifting pyramid means we need to stop viewing developing countries as passive beneficiaries of aid. Instead, we must listen to, assist, and elevate struggling *communities* within each country—even those in middle- and high-income countries. This change in focus means activists will work much more closely with local groups, responding to their demands for agency and self-determination. It means thinking about our "customers" very differently.

3. Equity. Leveling the field for people of all genders, races and ethnicities, sexual orientations, and disabilities has been reignited as a promising frontier in development. How activists engage with different communities to ensure inclusion, diversity, and full participation will shape the agenda.

4. Digital disruption. New data tools and the digital revolution will accelerate social development across every sector, from health to agriculture, financial services, and education. These powerful new capabilities, properly harnessed, have the potential to supercharge well-being for many more people. But they bring challenging questions around privacy, ethics, bias, and misinformation.

5. The surprisingly sexy middle. The key to improving millions of lives long-term lies less in invention than scaling and adapting

proven innovations—in other words, the all-important journey between an inspired concept and its on-the-ground implementation. In many cases we have the tools and technology to make a difference, but they sit on laboratory shelves. What we need are more social activists focused on building out those ideas to connect with the daily lives of real communities.

We will explore these five concepts in detail, offering examples and suggesting how they might further the work of practical activists everywhere. My hope is that they also stimulate the vision of a new generation.

Pyramid to Diamond

How Human Progress Is Reshaping the Activist's Agenda

Things are bad, and it feels like they are getting worse, right? The rich are getting richer and the poor are getting poorer; and the number of poor just keeps increasing . . . . At least that's the picture that most Westerners see in the media and carry around in their heads. I call it the overdramatic worldview. It's stressful and misleading. In fact, the vast majority of the world's population lives somewhere in the middle of the income scale. . . . Their girls go to school, their children get vaccinated, they live in two-child families, and they want to go abroad on holiday, not as refugees. Step-by-step, year-by-year, the world is improving.
—Hans Rosling, Factfulness: Ten Reasons We're Wrong About the World, and Why Things Are Better Than You Think

ONSTAGE AT NEW YORK City's Four Seasons Hotel, standing before 300 of the world's largest institutional investors, is the last place in the world you might expect to see a person in my line of work. But there I was, in the fall of 2019, preparing to speak to a room full of

33

Wall Street heavyweights about alleviating poverty and improving human health. A tough gig, to put it mildly.

I'd just stepped off a plane from the Democratic Republic of Congo (DRC), and I was reeling. Only a few days before, I'd been in a makeshift border town a stone's throw from Zambia. A narrow road wended through the shrubs and cassava fields until, suddenly, there were miles of trucks parked one behind the other, forming the outskirts of a huge tent city. This settlement had cropped up along the only road leading from the DRC copper mines into Zambia, and eventually to South Africa. Because the trucks were often stopped at the border for days, negotiating permission to transport their copper to market, a fledgling economy had sprouted up to sell goods to the truckers. Incredibly, a million people had settled around this border checkpoint, primarily selling food and sex. Only a few days before my talk with the Wall Street financiers, I'd been visiting brothels to see women training one another to use female condoms. In blistering heat and overpowering smells, walking down muddy paths among endless rows of shacks and tents, the whole place reeked of desperation.

Now, standing onstage at the Four Seasons, I felt like I'd been transported to a different planet. Everyone in front of me (most of them men) wore a suit, and there I was—rumpled, exhausted, and jet-lagged after a multileg journey from Africa.

I'm an optimistic person by nature, confident that even a bit of progress begets a virtuous cycle. You give someone better health, and they can get a better job, feed their family more, send their kids to school, and so on. But the Congolese border town had rocked me. In a setting like that I couldn't help wondering whether global development programs were merely expensive Band-Aids. Where do you even begin to chip away at the layers and layers of misery?

I hadn't been invited to the Four Seasons to guilt wealthy financiers into action. My aim was to explain how our old model of the global economy was changing and where that opened new opportunities for the private sector. The scene in the DRC was part of that change too. So, I launched in.

"You came from Connecticut; I'm coming from Congo. You have ties and hair, I don't. But we're more alike than you think," I said. "You spend your day managing complex systems, looking at spreadsheets, and trying to maximize returns. That's exactly what I do. I look at metrics, try to make sense of trends, and decide where to make the best bet for the biggest gains—I'm just going for a different type of impact. But we're not so far apart."

We're all on this planet together, I reminded them, gently alluding to the effects of extreme economic inequity. "We in the social innovation sector have one piece of the answer," I said. "But you in the financial services space have another, and I think these pieces actually fit together. In fact, global economics is reshaping our world in a way that make our respective worlds more and more intertwined."

I was introducing them to something I call the pyramid-to-diamond phenomenon.

Traditionally, global development work has focused on the comparatively straightforward goal of helping "low-income" countries at the "bottom of the pyramid" graduate out of poverty. The pyramid concept is derived from a simple graphic showing the distribution of wealth around the world: it has long been concentrated in the hands of very few rich countries and individuals at the top of an imaginary pyramid, while the vast majority of world's citizens—billions of people in more than a hundred nations—lived for centuries at "the bottom of the pyramid." Throughout most of human history, at least two-thirds of all people have lived in extreme poverty.

But today's global economy has become much more complex. The top economic group, as defined by both measurable income and wealth, has pulled away from the bottom, so that today a mere 1 percent of the global population controls more than half of the world's wealth. That trend appears to be accelerating. A recent report from the UK parliament suggests that this accumulation of wealth by the richest people on the planet will increase to 64 percent by 2030. According to Oxfam, 26 families control as much capital as the poorest 50 percent of the world's population. Visually, these trends look like a narrowing spike stretching taller and taller atop our old pyramid.

All true, and troubling. But these reports usually fail to explore the truly momentous change happening at the bottom, where data is harder to obtain and analyze, likely because those populations have always been less interesting to the marketers and financial institutions that study these trends. Sure, there are still more people at the bottom half than the top, and there are still too many people living in acute, chronic poverty at the bottom tip of the diamond—like those in that DRC border town. However, during the past 50 years, economic growth spurred by market forces, government policies, and aid programs has lifted hundreds of millions of people out of destitution and into the ranks of a new, low-income consumer class. In 2016, Brookings reported that the world had reached a tipping point, with over half of the globe's population now "middle class" with some discretionary spending power for the very first time. Worldwide, the middle class is expanding at rates faster than we've seen in human history; about 160 million people move up the pyramid to join those ranks each year. By 2030, that middle band is expected to swell to 5.3 billion people—1.7 billion more than it holds today. Meanwhile, the number of those wavering in the "vulnerable" zone between poverty and the middle class is projected to shrink by 900 million. Every single day, about 170,000 people move out of abject poverty.

This is why we should stop clinging to our old idea of the pyramid. It's just not accurate. The global economy has stretched into a squat diamond with a wide bottom and a skinny spire—kind of like a spinning top with a very narrow handle. It is happening unevenly and inequitably, but as the global health expert Hans Rosling wrote, "Step-by-step, year-by-year, the world is improving."

Pyramid to diamond. I see this transformation playing out almost everywhere I travel: in emerging urban neighborhoods brimming with scrappy entrepreneurs; in technology-driven industries that sit alongside slums or just outside poor villages; in new schools, hospitals, transit systems, and power grids serving communities that formerly had nothing; and across fast-growing markets in India, Brazil, Ethiopia, Peru, South Africa, Senegal, and beyond.

Back in 1979, when I first lived abroad in Asia, I never could have imagined this. At the time, China's poor accounted for almost half of the bottom of the pyramid, a broad tranche of people living on less than a dollar a day. Today, that China is barely a memory. In a single decade, from the mid-1980s to mid-1990s, China lifted more than 600 million people out of poverty and into the middle class—a phenomenal achievement, with resulting improvements in health and educational attainment that few people thought possible. In 2019, though China still had 16.6 million people living on less than $1.90 a day, the number was way down from the 100 million people suffering with that status in 2012. Chinese leaders have vowed to bring it all the way to zero in a few years. At the same time, 500 of the world's newest billionaires are Chinese.

Consider the economy of Vietnam, once among the weakest on the planet, which has grown by more than 5 percent each year for the past two decades. Or the 23 nations in Africa now on the World Bank's growing list of Middle-Income Countries with a Gross Domestic Product (GDP) per capita between US$1,026 and $12,475. That kind of economic growth has profound social reverberations. In India, under-five child mortality rates plummeted 30 percent between 2012 and 2018. In Myanmar, the life expectancy for women has been extended by 15 years since 1990.

Of course, the pyramid-to-diamond undercurrent does not diminish the immense suffering and unfairness that persist in distressed communities around the globe. Being a destitute kid on the streets of Damascus, Dakar, Delhi, or Detroit remains horrific, and unacceptable. There are still failed governments unable to address the basic needs of their citizens, a distressing number of states besieged by regional conflict and war, more refugees than the world has seen since World War II, and a new surge in authoritarian leadership worldwide—not to mention the crisis of climate change, its consequences for the world's poor, or the rise of new strains of disease like Ebola and the novel coronavirus, which disproportionately harm the most vulnerable. The upshot? While many global citizens are benefiting from growing socioeconomic progress, others are not. And their lot in life is possibly more dire than ever. That is where would-be social activists should consider leaning in.

So why would a practical activist want to explain this to a bunch of Wall Street types? Central to my work is the idea that most of our major global challenges—health, education, inclusive growth, climate change—can be solved only through partnerships between private enterprise, public agencies, and the philanthropic funders, nonprofits, and research organizations collectively referred to as the social sector. Our fast-morphing diamond—with its implications for expanded markets and new consumers—makes such multisector efforts much more possible.

This is not a new concept. In the early 2000s, books like *The Fortune at the Bottom of the Pyramid*, by management scholar C. K. Prahalad, began to talk about viewing the world's poor as a business opportunity, rather than merely a drain. Paul Collier, in *The Bottom Billion*, popularized the idea that the "BoP" (for "bottom of the pyramid") could be turned into a market for programs, interventions, and aid organizations. In other words, the poor could be seen as a new type of consumer—not people who would pay market rate for goods and services, but communities that nevertheless represented untapped possibility for positive social and economic benefits. As Prahalad wrote, "When the poor at the BoP are treated as consumers, they can reap the benefits of respect, choice, and self-esteem and have the opportunity to climb out of the poverty trap." Moreover, the emerging market opportunities presented by this fast-growing base of new consumers offers even more incentive for businesses and investors to engage in global development efforts. That, in broad strokes, is what I wanted to explain to the Wall Street set in New York City.

To be fair, I had a great entrée at the Four Seasons: Joel Holsinger, a very successful alternative credit investor who'd become interested in PATH's impact. He'd come from humble beginnings and wrestled on a personal level with questions around global inequity, so Joel began doing what he does best—researching hundreds of organizations, analyzing their impact, and learning all he could about making smart investments in global health. He had read every available PATH annual report before contacting us and had many great questions and ideas about our work. He became a champion of our efforts, later joining PATH's board, and he'd invited me to speak to his colleagues and clients gathered at the Four Seasons investors' meeting.

Already, Joel had done much to forge multisector opportunities. He'd convinced his partners at Ares Management to create a charitable donation from a portion of the carry and management fees they charged investors, putting that money toward global health and education. It's only a nascent effort today, but over the next five years that fund could grow to tens of millions of dollars in unrestricted money, which would have a huge impact on programs in the developing world.

It's easy to view this kind of partnership cynically, as a painless way for the affluent to assuage guilt or "give back" without really doing much of anything. But for many wealthy people like Joel, interest in global development comes from a broader perspective. They acknowledge that extreme income inequality—for which Wall Street wealth is often a poster child—is unsustainable. Many also perceive, correctly, that their insights as results-oriented businesspeople could be valuable. Most are smart and well-meaning—often grown-up versions of my students at Stanford—and talking with them about inequality resonates because no matter how much money you have, at the end of the day lots of people can't help asking themselves, "Have I really made the world any better?"

I understood some things about this audience. After spending much of my career in the for-profit world, running a tech company and serving on the boards of several multinational corporations, I knew well the tug-of-war discussions between an emphasis on profit and the simultaneous interest in social impact between shareholders and other kinds of stakeholders. As a veteran of both worlds—corporate and nonprofit—I believe both have an important role in social change. More to the point, I am convinced that boosting effective collaboration between business and the social sector will be critical over the next decade for any activist working to improve global equity.

Much has been written about the opportunities, challenges, and different models associated with private sector involvement in social change, and I've spent much of my career championing it. But I recognize that, for some, it can be an awkward pairing. One of the biggest hurdles to overcome is preconceived ideas. Over the years, I've seen knee-jerk attitudes sour potential collaboration again and again, with beliefs like: "nonprofits are inefficient and ineffective, unlike business"; or "businesspeople are greedy and selfish"; or "government employees are lazy." These biases constantly impede effective partnerships, though they tend to evaporate once people link arms and work together. Not that this kind of bridge-building is easy to do. Whatever the motives of those who engage with this work—whether it's an interest in the growing markets, a belief that vast inequity is untenable, a desire to apply their talents and resources to help others, or guilt about privilege—I've seen cross-sector collaborations result in powerful progress and change.

Our new, fat-diamond world means much more than simply engaging business in the work of social impact. It is making many of the basic assumptions around which global development was shaped increasingly outdated. The most important lesson is to stop thinking about this work as something that happens only in poor countries. Rather, activists must focus on helping poor or marginalized *communities* everywhere to rise. In the coming decades, social activism will be built increasingly around community-driven needs and challenges, whether those communities are in rich countries or poor.

Few nations demonstrate this phenomenon as clearly as India, projected soon to become the most populous country on earth. I spent a year there, running PATH's country-wide programs, and I saw the middle class growing at breakneck speed—it more than doubled in the eight years between 2004 and 2012, according to economists at Mumbai University. (They defined middle class as people spending anywhere between US$2 and $10 per capita each day.) More than half of India's 1.3 billion people are now part of this strengthening demographic, including many street vendors, farmers, and urban slum-dwellers.

However, in the midst of the growing GDP, pockets of acute need persist. Some have even gotten worse. In the large northern state of Bihar, which has a population of nearly 100 million, PATH is working with the state government to vaccinate people who subsist on beetles dug from the earth. Many children are stunted, there is little water, few jobs, and kids still die of vaccine-preventable diseases at an outrageous rate—this, in a middle-class nation of increasing wealth, where most of the world's public sector vaccines are made. The dichotomies, to put it mildly, are striking.

You'll find similar contrasts in Africa, as well as in rich countries like the United States and the UK. In Hartford, Connecticut, nicknamed "the Insurance Capital of the World" and home to the $60.5 billion Aetna Corporation, nearly 40 percent of households live on less than $25,000 a year. In Seattle, where I live, homeless camps sprawl beside almost every luxury condominium, and median life expectancy can vary up to 12 years, depending on zip code (often correlating to race and ethnicity). Increasingly, whether in the United States, Ethiopia, India, or anywhere else, indicators of well-being are directly associated with the resources of your particular micro-community.

For all these reasons, global development and activism can no longer be thought of as *country*-specific, but rather *community*-specific. And that necessitates major changes to how we think about serving people in need. It means moving away from dated concepts born of the twentieth century's post-colonial paradigm, where the so-called "global north" acted with a sort of noblesse oblige toward the "global south." Going forward, we will need to focus on struggling populations within each country because we now live in a world where many of the poorest communities exist in middle- or even high-income nations. It also means that global activists will need to engage with countries of all income levels.

You can see growing evidence of this change in new policies. Look at the United Nations' Sustainable Development Goals (SDGs) approved by all member states of the UN in 2015. These new goals and their 2030 deadline very intentionally reframe the UN's earlier development aims—which focused on poor countries—to make poverty alleviation, gender equity, and climate action the obligation of *all* nations, rich and poor.

And at Gavi, the global vaccine alliance to improve access to new and underused vaccines for children, policies mandate that countries "graduate" the program as they become wealthier. Yet, because a higher per-capita GDP does not mean poverty is eradicated or the need for subsidized immunization programs goes away, Gavi structures these transitions to ensure that poor communities continue to get what they need—even in countries where economies are strengthening. Since its founding in 2000, Gavi has helped to vaccinate more than 760 million children and has prevented more than 13 million deaths.

This shift is playing out on the ground across nearly every continent, with more focus on reaching marginalized populations and encouraging new models for entrepreneurism. More exciting still, many of these communities are finding the voice to demand what they need, rather than passively accepting whatever they get.

In Vietnam, for instance, the gay community had long been pushed to the shadows. This created a disaster when AIDS hit. The first case of HIV was reported in December 1990, in Saigon. By 2002, 12 years later, there were more than 104,000 new infections, mainly due to stigma around buying condoms. By 2005, an estimated 263,000 Vietnamese were living with HIV or AIDS—though many were unaware. The numbers were spiking in three high-risk groups: IV-drug users, sex workers, and men who had sex with men (MSM). (The term, used widely in global health, reflects the broad group of men at risk, many of whom do not necessarily identify with the LGBTQI community.)

Vietnam is a socially conservative country—one government agency is called the Department of Social Evils Prevention—and its health ministry had focused its anti-HIV efforts only on IV-drug users, with outreach efforts consisting primarily of skull-and-crossbones posters. Sex workers and gay men were ignored. As a result, HIV rates soared in the early 2000s—some estimates suggested the virus was afflicting up to 18 percent of urban populations. But only 30 percent of those in the three high-risk groups were actually getting tested, since diagnosis was available only at government offices. (The stigma alone discouraged most people from learning their status; for many, a positive diagnosis paled in comparison with the potential for being ostracized by family.) Referral rates for treatment were even worse. Yet the Ministry of Health announced plans to eradicate the disease by 2030.

The ambition was understandable, given its context. Vietnam, once one of the world's poorest nations, had transformed itself into a growing economic power in just 25 years. By 2010, it had officially ascended to middle-income status, and the economy was on fire. But this stunning turnaround created an unexpected problem.

As the country grew stronger economically, longtime donors like the Global Fund to Fight AIDS, Malaria, and Tuberculosis began to cut back on their financial commitments. The United States' PEP-FAR (President's Emergency Plan for AIDS Relief) program had once provided 80 percent of Vietnam's funding for HIV/AIDS prevention. But PEPFAR also curbed its outlay. Smaller donors like Australia, the UK, and the Ford Foundation pulled out completely. In all, Vietnam's economic success cost it more than $1 billion in outside funding for HIV/AIDS prevention and treatment.

Dynamic as its economy was, that kind of money was more than the Vietnamese government could comfortably make up. What to do? On the one hand, you had the extraordinary success story of a country decimated by war building itself into an economic power-house; on the other, a looming health crisis. Within this gap, the seeds of an answer took root, one that married Vietnam's emerging entrepreneurialism with the needs of the hard-to-reach gay community. It also happened to intersect with the personal journey of a gay man from Ho Chi Minh City.

In 2014, the U.S. Agency for International Development (USAID), reshaping its programs around the new pyramid-to-diamond dynamic, began looking for ideas that could create "economically sustainable" approaches to fighting HIV. It wanted a means to involve the private sector and encourage domestic financing, rather than reliance on donor funds. Winning proposals would generate more demand and new service models for testing, treatment, and prevention. The name of this effort was "Healthy Markets," neatly encapsulating its social and economic aims.

At the time, a young man named Le Minh Thanh was reluctantly headed for a career in law. Well-educated, he had been born into a middle-class family and was expected to fall in line socially—with a wife, children, and conventional career. But that was not how Thanh saw himself. He identified as gay, though his parents did not know it, and his overriding passion was supporting his community.

For several years, Thanh met quietly with a handful of like-minded activists to talk about AIDS prevention. He called their small group Glink. Its mission: to reach gay men in Ho Chi Minh City who were hiding their sexual identity and educate them about the disease. In 2015, Thanh applied for a small grant through the Healthy Markets program to do HIV outreach and prevention in a more organized manner. He turned out to be a genius at using social media for those ends, recognizing that Facebook offered a discreet, direct way to reach potential clients for his slowly growing nonprofit.

Meanwhile, the Vietnamese government had passed groundbreaking legislation that allowed laypeople to do testing. Suddenly, you didn't need to go to a doctor's office to find out if you were HIV-positive. Someone like Thanh could do it for you in a community clinic. The following year, he opened one, the first gay-managed private clinic in the country. Housed in a generic-looking office building, there were no rainbow flags, posters, or anything that suggested "gayness" about Glink. The clinic looked like it could have been a trading company—clean, crisp, and bland. But it sold condoms, offered 24-hour counseling, and provided testing, anti-retroviral therapy, and post- and pre-exposure prophylaxis. Simultaneously, the team at PATH was training Thanh, along with leaders from eight similar community groups, on business skills and leadership.

This confluence of a growing economy and support for community efforts changed everything. "The community sees us as the go-to now!" soft-spoken Thanh was suddenly telling our staff with excitement. "We don't have to chase them—everyone is coming to us!"

His newfound confidence was unmistakable. But Thanh was more than just a community activist. He had the vision of an entrepreneur. Three years after I met him, he'd opened four new clinics and expanded to offer services for gay men suffering from hypertension and Hepatitis C.

Today, Glink and the eight other community leaders nurtured by Healthy Markets to become social entrepreneurs employ dozens of people. They have built thriving partnerships with medical supply firms that sell them condoms, needles, and prophylactic medication, and they are reaching thousands of people with testing, treatment, and education. Most of all, these community activists-turned-businessmen are curbing the spread of HIV. Back in 2004, such a venture would have been flat-out crazy. The idea of a grassroots community group building itself into a profitable company, inconceivable.

The Healthy Markets program has demonstrated enormous successes, both medically and economically. Condom sales in Vietnam more than quintupled in two years—from 5 million units in 2015 to nearly 28 million in 2017. And all nine of the original community groups supported by the program have become licensed healthcare providers, though none was founded by a medical professional. Total profits for these nine businesses increased by 52 percent between 2016 and 2018, and Thanh's Glink chain now operates five sites across Vietnam—a staggering leap from his original outpost in an out-of-the-way alley. Another Healthy Markets clinic forecasts a customer base expanded by 30 percent in 2020. I cannot think of a more inspiring example to demonstrate the potential for innovation in global development.

But none of it would have been possible without Vietnam's rise into the middle class. Thanh knew that his clients would be willing and able to pay something for services, and that enabled businesses to sell him and the other Healthy Markets clinics condoms at a low cost so they could begin building their bottom line. This critical shift—to thinking about targeted communities as consumers and not beneficiaries—is an important ripple arising from the pyramid-to-diamond undercurrent. In the first half of 2019, the private sector in Vietnam invested more than $2 million to help combat HIV—while making a profit. No longer are Glink patients and the gay community overall viewed as passive recipients of aid. Instead, they are customers—demanding value, providing feedback, shaping markets, and mastering their own destinies.

This kind of turnaround is not unique to Vietnam. Thanh has joined a growing group of emerging-economy businesspeople around the world, who see entrepreneurialism as a way of eradicating bottom-of-the-pyramid inequality through the virtuous cycle that profit creates. In the next chapter, I'll offer another example of the way small business healthcare providers in an urban slum became essential for curbing the spread of tuberculosis in India. But here's a preview: the phenomenon of communities becoming customers is an important undercurrent all its own.

Growing markets at the bottom of the diamond is evident in brilliant programs like Africa's One Acre Fund, which offers an $80 bundle of services—including quality seeds, fertilizer, tutorials on modern agricultural techniques, and training on market fluctuations—to smallholder farmers, on credit. In 2017, One Acre reported that it had served 600,000 farmers in eight countries, most of whom realized returns of more than 200 percent. Ninety-eight percent had been able to repay their loans.

For social activists, the undercurrent represented by these stories should point to the critical need for increased incentives around collaboration with the private sector. As economies grow, providing services to people in the lower-middle of the diamond will offer opportunities for business of all sizes—from traditional farmers and local entrepreneurs to regional and national firms—even multinationals. More small businesses like Li Minh Thanh's Glink clinics are finding ways to serve consumers in the "squat" part of the diamond—to do good and do well at once. Large multinational corporations like Unilever and Royal Philips—each of which is developing products focused on this emerging high-volume, low-margin consumer base—are increasingly visible in these markets and committed to doing more to help these communities. Other large companies, like the African wireless provider Econet and the Indian conglomerate Tata, are building shared-value programs to serve low-income communities profitably, while simultaneously setting up generous philanthropies And Novartis, a leading pharmaceutical company based in Switzerland, has developed a subscription model for 20 essential medicines provided to some low-income communities at about $1 per month. The trend appears irreversible as demographics shift, markets grow, and new opportunities arise.

Yet another effect of the pyramid-to-diamond undercurrent is the rapidly changing landscape for global development resources, beyond market engagement. Take China, arguably the largest single donor of aid dollars in the world, even exceeding the United States (although the numbers are difficult to measure, given the opacity of Chinese foreign assistance data). China adopted its One Belt One Road Policy, a global development strategy to build infrastructure and investment in nearly 70 countries and international organizations, 2013. Many in the West have criticized One Belt One Road as an aggressive attempt to extend China's economic and political influence across Asia and Africa. But it is a natural outgrowth of the shifting pyramid, which has created new donors in Africa and India who have their own agendas. Extend the pattern and it's not hard to see how the entire tradition of development dictated by Geneva, New York, London, and even Seattle (as home of the world's largest philanthropic foundation) could soon be recalibrated, with the BRICS (Brazil, Russia, India, China, and South Africa) and other countries wielding much greater influence on social activism everywhere.

An increased role for the BRICS, and other countries, will reach beyond their strengthening finances. On almost every project that PATH undertakes, it is standard practice to look to India, China, South Africa, Brazil, Indonesia, and other countries for partnership possibilities or ideas for finding cost-effective ways to accelerate health innovation. In PATH's extensive vaccine development programs, these global partners are critical. Take Japanese encephalitis (JE), for example. This is a disease that mostly affects poor, rural people across Southeast Asia and the Western Pacific. Caused by a virus transmitted by mosquitoes, JE can lead to serious brain infection with long-term—often fatal—consequences. Children are at the greatest risk of dying from JE, and those who survive often suffer permanent neurological disabilities, like paralysis and the inability to speak. And because there is no cure, protection through vaccination is the most realistic way to protect communities.

But when researchers at PATH decided to tackle JE, they discovered that every vaccine on the exiting public health market was too expensive for many low-income countries. Even when available, they required multiple doses and posed safety risks—all of which meant that most vulnerable populations remained unprotected. There was one manufacturer, however, who was making a safe, effective, and affordable vaccine—in China.

The Chinese had been using their JE vaccine for nearly 20 years, protecting 200 million children. Yet this intervention was not widely available beyond China's borders. Nor could it be, because the vaccine lacked an essential prequalification by the WHO. Getting that stamp of approval is mandatory for access to the public sector and scaling up any immunization program in low-income countries.

But after an outbreak of JE in 2005 killed thousands of people in India and Nepal, PATH stepped up its efforts to find ways of fast-tracking the Chinese vaccine. What the WHO needed, first, was data, an evidence base arguing for the vaccine's wider use. Officers at PATH began building a relationship with the Chinese vaccine manufacturer, the Chengdu Institute of Biological Products, to develop that information. This took years. It meant designing clinical trials, building factories that could triple the output of doses, and negotiating affordable prices. In 2013 the WHO granted this JE vaccine the first-ever prequalification for a Chinese-made inoculation. As a result, more than 300 million children across Asia have been protected.

The partnership also opened the door to global procurement and new financing mechanisms for low-income countries. Just as important, the prequalification symbolized China's entry as a major player in global public health.

As the COVID-19 pandemic has made vividly clear, our world will need a lot more of this cross-border partnering if we're going to address the looming health, environmental, and development challenges coming at us. COVID-19 has also illustrated the irony of a world order turning upside down. In global health scenarios during the past century, almost all epidemic planning done by U.S. agencies focused on helping other countries address their outbreaks. Of course, there had been domestic responses to various flus and viruses, like Zika, but most models for pandemic preparedness were designed around eruptions elsewhere. They were almost entirely directed at containment—that is, keeping a disease from reaching the shores of Europe and America. The coronavirus turned all of that on its head.

While it likely originated in China, the United States and Europe quickly became disease epicenters. Woefully unprepared and lacking adequate supplies, the globe's biggest economies were desperately turning to South Asia, Mexico, and other parts of the world for support—a stunning turnabout. The global crisis has also spotlighted vulnerable communities in every country around the world—in this instance, not just the poorest among us, but also the elderly and sick.

During the crisis, Alex Ng, a brilliant medical doctor from New Zealand (who also has a degree in health informatics), provided an inspiring example of what's possible when private enterprise works with government for the public good. I knew Alex through his work at McKinsey and the Gates Foundation's office in Beijing. But when COVID-19 struck, he was the vice president of Tencent Healthcare, the giant Chinese tech company in Hong Kong. Alex's life became 24/7 COVID. His team at Tencent developed an ingenious WeChat-based application to track the outbreak, share information for communities, create surveillance tools for health officials, and link data to government sources in an interoperable manner. The overarching concept was to use this information for shaping a strategy as the number of patients began to subside and people started returning to work. While Tencent is a private company, Alex and other leaders there were committed to sharing its capabilities as a public good. They were not alone. Many organizations—private, public, and social—began sharing tools, ideas, intellectual property, and talent to address the pandemic and its cascading effects.

This response also underscored the incredible power within the private sector to step up its involvement with practical activism in profound ways. I had a close-up view, helping organize digital technology companies to combat the epidemic by volunteering employees and resources so they could assist with global priorities established by the WHO. At the same time, we saw an abundance of so-called "reverse innovation"—ideas for fighting COVID-19 moving from the global south to the global north—which will create more opportunity within the lower bands of our world's economic diamond. And as the supply of masks, gowns, respirators, and other medical equipment shrank to frighteningly low levels in Europe and the United States, entrepreneurs in Mexico, India, and Indonesia—as well as small businesses in North America and Europe—retooled to answer the demand. Suddenly, practical activists were no longer delivering services or shaping programs for export to the global south. They were addressing problems at home, working behind the scenes to equip hospitals, build communication, and support people in self-quarantine. Working alongside the political leaders in Washington State to source medical supplies, we found ourselves partnering with brokers and companies across the developing world. In all—between pooling talent, offering new apps to track the disease, and deploying artificial intelligence to more quickly discover new drugs—the amount of private sector innovation pouring into the COVID-19 response from all corners of the globe was unprecedented.

Put plainly, we are in a new world. Today, China, India, and most of South America and Eastern Europe are standing on their own, with little need of the type of assistance we in the global north provided throughout the twentieth century. Does this mean there is no more need for global development? Hardly. It means that global development must change. What countries require now is assistance of a very different kind. Our role and influence may be smaller in scope, and our end goal a handoff, rather than permanent residence.

It is undeniably an exciting time. But a diamond-shaped world also raises uncomfortable new questions: Who is shaping global policies and programs now? Should the United States, the UK, and traditional big donors continue to provide aid to India and other ascendant countries? (Though India's GDP, at $2.6 trillion, is a thousand times bigger than 30 years ago, it still has the largest number of chronically poor people in the world.) Should we reevaluate the metrics by which countries and communities are measured? The Gini coefficient, for example, measures wealth distribution as a gauge of inequality. The Human Development Index offers a composite of life expectancy, education, and income indicators. Are these more appropriate models? How do we support human development considering the impact that growing affluence will have on climate, food supply, and other limited resources? Do these trends portend a bifurcated world of the future, made up of middle- and high-income communities continuing to see gains in health and development, while fragile states remain locked in cycles of poverty and conflict requiring constant humanitarian relief and never advancing? Some influencers suggest exactly that. Either way, these questions will spur debates that all practical activists need to engage with—while still getting the work done.

There is, as well, an ugly underside as our old pyramid stretches into a diamond: the widening gulf between this planet's very richest and poorest people—sometimes living in adjacent communities.

We see this frequently in the United States, where a bulging middle class has made the country diamond-shaped for decades, even as homeless families camp outside of luxury condos. The chasm between our ultra-rich and desperately poor leaves those at the bottom quartile trapped for generations on the lower rungs of the economic ladder, with less and less opportunity to advance.

This vastly more globalized, middle-class world also represents significant disruption to traditional power relationships. The old standard of wealthy countries doling out largesse to (and winning concessions from) recipients of aid will gradually fall away as the "decolonization" of global health and development occurs. More and more, this new world order will require ceding power to local groups, who know what they need and don't want to be told what to do. It will shift our framework away from being beneficent donors in perpetuity and toward something closer to project-based consultants. That is a potentially momentous change. But making it stick will require engagement of private sector partners at every level—from frontline providers to social enterprises, local companies, and multinational corporations.

The work ahead of us now is to build on this momentum and accelerate its progress. In lectures around the world, I frequently urge students, colleagues, and activists to continue "bending the curve"—on poverty reduction, child mortality, illiteracy, and preventable vaccine deaths. We'll need a lot of talent and innovation to do that—not to mention some new ideas for places where the trendlines aren't great. But overall, our morphing global diamond is a powerful undercurrent that will carry humanity forward. If there is anything that should move activists from outrage to optimism, this is it.

Communities Are the Customers

How Activists Must Heed the Voices and Demands of Communities

There is no power for change greater than a community discovering what it cares about.

—Margaret J. Wheatley, American author on leadership

In the teeming Dharavi slum of Mumbai, a 17-year-old girl named Rabiya had a nagging pain in her shoulder. Her family thought it might be a pulled muscle. But Rabiya also developed breathlessness, and the pain got worse. Not far away, in the same overcrowded urban ward, a laborer ignored his persistent cough. Another worker, the only breadwinner in his family, grimaced through unaccountable back pain, unable to sleep until, finally, he skipped a day's work to visit a folk healer. The diagnosis—tuberculosis—didn't require much guesswork. More than two million people in India were suffering from the fatal disease in 2011, most of them living shoulder to shoulder in Mumbai's impoverished slums. That's a public health nightmare. But there was worse to come.

"Incurable TB an Epidemic?" screamed multiple newspaper headlines across the country that year. The fear was entirely reasonable. India had become one of the largest middle-income countries in the world, and Mumbai was its financial center, a city of millionaires and slum-dwellers, the latter susceptible to diseases that could spread like wildfire, affecting all.

Among all the world's infectious diseases, tuberculosis is by far the biggest killer. And in Mumbai, the fifth most populous city on the planet, about nine million people live in the poorest wards, where makeshift shacks and old apartment buildings cram together along a maze of teeming streets and garbage-strewn alleyways. People come and go without fixed mailing addresses, often traveling to rural villages for seasonal work and returning when those jobs disappear. In that scenario, you can see how difficult it might be to keep track of who is sick, let alone who's been treated and which treatments are working—or not.

These logistical problems were made worse by traditions around healthcare in these slums. Rather than going to a government hospital for diagnosis and treatment, about 70 percent of ward residents prefer to visit private practitioners—in the West they might be called alternative medicine providers—who have varying degrees of medical training, access to testing, and front-line drugs. In their storefront clinics, patients may wait in a jam-packed room, coughing for hours before being evaluated. And in 2011, with these private providers treating hundreds of patients a day, it was difficult to ensure that each was being properly diagnosed and completing a full course of medication to halt the disease.

The result of this haphazard treatment was twofold: a new strain of tuberculosis had developed that was impervious to standard treatment, and each sick person might infect dozens more before their illness was treated or fully cured. Thus, the government concern.

What to do? How to convince millions of poor people to abandon their neighborhood practitioners and instead go to government hospitals they neither liked nor trusted or could afford? The practitioners themselves had little incentive to encourage this change, since whenever they followed the rules and reported contagious patients, government physicians effectively penalized them by removing the client (and related revenues).

A traditional global health response would involve convening committees of global experts in faraway places like Geneva, Washington, DC, or London, devising a strategy and deploying a fleet of workers to flood the region with outside expertise, often at great cost. This is the kind of response we saw in programs like the United States' President's Emergency Plan for AIDS Relief (PEPFAR), an enormously ambitious, global effort with targets and interventions managed out of Washington, DC. Similarly, world health leaders mobilized an outside-in, blanket-the-region approach to fight Ebola virus in Africa. While these top-down approaches have been successful in curbing HIV and quashing a harrowing epidemic, neither model was going to work in Mumbai, where a rapidly spreading disease affected millions of people living in close quarters.

Dr. Shibu Vijayan, PATH's expert on the ground, was convinced the answer lay in devising a plan that linked the slums' private practitioners to the government's more uniform, trackable medical system. But it would mean abandoning the usual big-bureaucracy approach and devising incentives that aligned with the community. The answer was to create a new organization, the Private Provider Interface Agency, to send trained field workers—most from the neighborhoods—into the street to gain the trust of the community providers. The program, led by local government and a consortium of partners, conceived a clever way to negotiate the financial disincentive that had previously discouraged the community providers. Each time they sent coughing patients to a government-approved lab for chest X-rays, the service was free, and if the images suggested

TB, patients would be referred to a hospital for diagnosis, also free of charge. Drug prescriptions were fulfilled back in the neighborhood, at a storefront pharmacist who would send a nominal kickback back to the practitioner—again covered by the government. And if the TB was drug-resistant, patients would be sent to a government hospital at no cost. To ensure that the sick completed their full nine-month treatment cycle, prescription refills would be tracked, with a call center contracted to text patients and "nudge" them toward finishing the course.

This elaborate plan met with great skepticism when it launched in 2014. Would Mumbai's untrained storefront practitioners participate faithfully? Would patients follow through? Would all this effort result in better care, lower infections, and manageable costs?

The short answers are yes, yes, and yes. A 2019 study funded by PATH, World Health Partners, and the Bill & Melinda Gates Foundation found that the Mumbai pilot cost the government less than it had already budgeted for TB control, while vastly improving case management. From 2014 to 2019, the project diagnosed and tracked over 60,000 new cases of tuberculosis, mainly through these private caregivers who increased reporting eightfold. Nudged along through call center contacts and text messaging, more than 50,000 of those patients are now disease-free, and over 43,000 patients with challenging drug-resistant varieties of TB have begun more complex treatment regimens. Results have been so promising that state governments across the country are now replicating it in 32 other cities. ReAct, an international network of scientists focused on antibiotic resistance, hailed the model as one that could make a dent in reducing multidrug resistance to numerous diseases.

You have likely noted some of the unusual aspects of this solution to a dauntingly complex problem. It forged a network linking the public and private sectors. It used a simple technology (text messages) to help patients with compliance. Most important, it met patients where they were, respecting their medical traditions and relationships with neighborhood practitioners. And it was tailored to work for the realities of a particular community—the slums of Mumbai—at the direction of local government and community leaders, rather than relying on an elaborate, expensive, outsider-designed response that would be difficult to maintain if donors moved on to another project. It worked *with* the community, rather than *on* it.

This last aspect—a community-centered approach—was key to the project's success, and it exemplifies an important undercurrent accelerating across global development.

Community-centered activism is not new. It has been around, in one form or another, as long as there have been communities. But its growing prominence in global activism is truly transformative. As more countries ascend from the bottom of the pyramid into lower- and middle-income status, communities within each are seizing the reins to shape their own destinies. This represents a significant departure from the way global activism has worked traditionally.

Global development, as practiced today, relies on an architecture created during the post–World War II period, when there was tremendous need among developing nations (many emerging from colonialism) and a capacity among the victors to provide it. Seventy-five years later, aid programs remain anchored in large European and American-based organizations, which still drive the agenda. But very often those efforts, well-intended as they may be, play out on the ground as outdated, inappropriate, or tone-deaf—shipping large tractors to Africa, where much farming is done on small, hillside landholdings; or providing drugs and vaccines to supplement (but, really, replace) traditional healing methods; or parachuting in foreign students to teach while failing to align their work with local strategies. In our morphing pyramid-to-diamond world, where more countries have the infrastructure and capability to steer aspects of their own growth, these outside-in, top-down models feel increasingly outmoded.

Mumbai was a bold step toward something quite different. PATH and its partners engaged there at the community's invitation. We listened to its various constituencies. We embraced its customs and hired its workers, bending to their needs, rather than expecting the reverse. As the project progressed, we adapted to questions and concerns, working from the neighborhood out, not from the outside in. This idea of placing the community, family, or person at the center of activism is an important trend in social change, and I believe it will accelerate.

Precisely what does it mean to be community-centered? First, it starts from the ground up, with a lot of listening to learn about the values, needs, and challenges of a particular region, then designing a response tailored to fit. This sounds obvious, maybe elementary. But it requires admitting that we, as outsiders, do not have all the answers. It means proceeding with a certain humility and willingness to adapt, rather than imposing solutions from on high. It means focusing on understanding and meeting communities' demands, rather than developing programs based on the existing supply of products or ideas.

The best way to illustrate how this concept plays out is to describe the standard route, which usually means marshaling a cohort of recognized experts who, from afar, design programs they will never need to use. Generally, these ideas are based on solid research and good intentions, often with critical input from local political, financial, or subject matter leaders (in health or education, for instance). PEPFAR, the U.S. government's flagship effort to fight HIV/AIDS around the world, is a classic example.

Credited with significantly curbing the HIV epidemic in Africa and saving some 18 million lives, PEPFAR was developed in 2003 by a team of top-notch global health experts convened by President George W. Bush. Managed from Washington, DC, and implemented across the world through partnerships with the U.S. Centers for Disease Control (CDC), the U.S. Agency for International Development (USAID), and other partners, PEPFAR is widely seen as one of the most effective global health programs in history. Its results have been indeed remarkable. PEPFAR focused on clear targets and accountability measures—essential for any development program. But over the years, partly because of its large footprint and top-down culture, those it serves have become increasingly reluctant to voice concerns about the places where it falls short. In the offices of community leaders across Africa and Asia, I frequently hear complaints about PEPFAR's abrupt and remote decision-making, its lack of sensitivity to local context, and its vertical model disconnected from local health systems and communities. More recently, PEPFAR has narrowed its original, 50-country scope to prioritize a small number of high-burden hotspots, raising fears about its responsiveness to the realities of our diamond-shaped world. For those reasons—not to mention its enormous $5 billion annual cost—I doubt if PEPFAR will serve as a development paradigm for the future, no matter how impressive its triumphs.

We saw similar concerns raised about the global response to Ebola virus outbreaks in the Democratic Republic of Congo (DRC). While there was obviously a need for outside help to combat this monstrous disease—not least, because it attacked in a part of the world with a very weak health infrastructure—there has been mounting criticism of the global north's command-and-control approach. In some communities, there was backlash so severe against the swarm of outside experts who descended that people attacked clinics and killed health workers, believing that these foreigners had implanted the disease. Then, just as WHO Director-General Tedros Adhanom Ghebreyesus (known as Dr. Tedros) was preparing to announce the DRC's "last case" of Ebola in April 2020, a new one appeared. Even in a tweet, Dr. Tedros's disappointment was evident. But I believe the entire global health sector has learned some lessons about the importance of getting community engagement upfront that will go a long way toward cooling the tensions that flare when a bunch of well-funded strangers show up in poor communities, telling people what to do.

"We need to engage local leadership, including local chiefs, and bring community groups on board with community conversations targeting caretakers and groups vulnerable to the virus," said Amy Daffe, Mercy Corps' deputy country director for the DRC, writing in 2019 about why the outbreak had been so difficult to control. Local buy-in was key, she noted, calling out the lack of effort that had gone into building trust on the ground. "Instead of working with local leaders, outsiders arrived spreading messages that have left communities with more questions than answers. Information has not been well-tailored to different community contexts nor appropriately adapted to local languages or social norms."

Ebola is endemic in Congo, Daffe concluded, pointing to the likelihood of future outbreaks. "The systems and awareness we establish now will not only save lives currently but also in the years to come. Only when communities are at the forefront of the response—with preparation, training, tools, support, and funding—will we be able to end this epidemic."

This disconnect is not a dynamic unique to efforts in the developing world or global health. Across the U.S. public education system, there have been similarly angry reactions against efforts like No Child Left Behind, which demanded that schools meet specific performance standards and tied those benchmarks to federal funding. The carrot-and-stick concept, passed by Congress in 2002, was intended to improve education for struggling students. But its centralized, one-size-fits-all model inspired a surge of resentment against standardized testing and education reform that reverberates to this day. Common Core—another well-intentioned effort to boost student outcomes during the Obama administration—also stumbled. Common Core sought to close widely acknowledged variances in quality between schools, districts, and states. It assembled impressive panels of curriculum experts to determine the skills and materials all students should master at a given grade level. There's nothing inherently wrong with that, yet the campaign failed to achieve these ambitions, primarily due to its top-down style. Most important, in developing its standards and plans, Common Core neglected to get broad buy-in from the people who would be most affected by them: teachers.

I am not arguing that high-level, centralized programs should disappear. In many cases—such as the novel coronavirus pandemic that began in late 2019—a large-scale, coordinated approach is absolutely necessary. Nor am I suggesting that there is no role for outside experts and support—whether to share ideas, provide technical assistance, or offer research that a community may lack. But aside from humanitarian relief scenarios, the pendulum is swinging more and more toward aid and development models where communities and *their* demands drive practical activism. As with Vietnam's Glink clinics mentioned in Chapter 2, this change is a natural outgrowth of the pyramid-to-diamond phenomenon, and practical activists would do well to support it.

All around us, this community-centered approach is taking off. The Stars Foundation, founded by Saudi businessman Amr Al-Dabbagh, used to award prizes to nonprofits in the developing world that were well structured and training their people to create stronger organizations. But Stars's officers realized that instead of rewarding the standouts, they could spread impact much farther by helping all community groups do better. So they pivoted, building Philanthropy University, a free online platform open to all community groups looking for training or a place to connect with others facing similar challenges, worldwide. Even with that global reach and technology platform, I consider Philanthropy University an example of community-centered development. It started with a commitment to put local needs and people at the center, supporting their ability to make social change themselves.

I saw a beautiful example of the way this can play out at a gritty, crowded truck stop in a remote region of Uttar Pradesh, India, in 2006. At the time, HIV rates in India were lower than those in many other places. But among truckers and sex workers cases were spiking, and the government worried that without intervention these high-risk groups might spur an explosion of the disease in the wider population. How to reach these highly mobile people, many of whom traveled under the radar and distrusted the government? The Avahan HIV-prevention project targeted distinct communities and reached them using tools that may sound surprising. I could hardly believe it when I saw a group of truckers—rough men dressed up in colorful costumes—doing street theater. But it was extraordinary. One man played the part of a befuddled driver; others, his cajoling friends. A few pretended to be female sex workers and quack doctors. Their unexpectedly hilarious skit—which presented the risks of HIV and methods for prevention without lecturing—was performed in front of a highly participatory audience, many of them fellow truckers. Incredibly, the performers were able to convey their extremely serious message with hysterical humor. Does it sound silly or soft? I can assure you, watching a community tell its own story was a far more effective way to disseminate information about behavior change than having some outsider stand there, handing out pamphlets.

Avahan has many components—street theater is but a small part—and because it is funded by the Gates Foundation, a heavyweight in global philanthropy, some might consider it a top-down effort. But Avahan was explicitly focused on working with at-risk communities at the grassroots level. In a country the size of India, that meant reaching about 300,000 people during the program's first three years. By the end of that period, 90 percent of those individuals had visited clinics—nearly quadrupling previous rates—and condom use was up.

"Why are you doing this?" I asked some of the street performers after their show.

"So many of us don't understand AIDS," the lead narrator said. "We hear all sorts of things, so we need to share this story. We want to help our friends."

"But why not have professional actors do it?"

"We would never believe them. We get told all the time by others how to drive, what to wear, what we can do, what we can't. We've stopped listening to the government."

Another piped up. "It's better if we learn and share with each other. Then we believe."

Behavior change, which is what this effort aimed to encourage, gets into dicey territory. Driven by outsiders, it can be easily interpreted as paternalistic or judgmental. Therefore, a community-based approach becomes particularly useful. When I was running PATH's India office, I heard about a group called Digital Green, which was helping smallholder farmers in rural India assist one another by sharing agricultural techniques through community-made videos shown in group meetings. The key was local growers helping each other, instead of trying to apply ideas pushed on them from outside. "These videos help us to do more," said farmer Invi Krishna, who learned that he could grow food organically—and more cheaply—by using cow dung and urine as pesticides. "If someone tells you how to do something, you hear it, but you don't always take it in."

Digital Green, which launched in 2008, appeared quite successful—it has now reached more than two million households—and it spurred an idea. Could people sharing tools and ideas with one another change behavior around health too?

I'd seen efforts to promote safer childbirth by printing information on posters and paper handouts. Visit any frontline medical clinic across Africa or South Asia, and you can't miss the diagrams papering waiting room walls. This literature—centrally developed and static—is evidence-based, but not terribly compelling. Which means it isn't very effective. When a respected public figure offers the same message, you'll see some improvement. That's why celebrities from Bollywood and Hollywood show up so often in public service campaigns. But by far the most trusted source of information about health, agriculture, and myriad other aspects of day-to-day life is a neighbor or friend—someone you know, someone you've spoken to for years. What if social innovation could leverage that power, my PATH colleagues thought, working with local influencers to spread the word? As a result, Digital Green and PATH co-developed a project, Projecting Health, to provide simple digital cameras and appropriate messages for rural Indian women to share safe-birthing practices with their neighbors.

We've used the same concept—community influencers—to dispel incorrect beliefs around polio vaccination, too. In recorded history, humans have fully eradicated only one disease: smallpox. But we are living in extraordinary times, within reach of wiping out guinea worm, sleeping sickness, malaria, and other devastating conditions. Among them, polio is the biggest prize. Philanthropists and Rotary clubs around the globe have been at the forefront of efforts to eradicate this truly awful disease. But that success, as always, depends on community buy-in, so working with tribal and faith-based leaders to encourage vaccination is key. I will never forget listening to Islamic scholars and imams at a global polio conference in Abu Dhabi affirm that vaccinating children was a holy act in the Quran—directly countermanding fatwas made by other Islamic leaders who believed (mistakenly) that polio vaccination would impair fertility. Some might also have forbidden it because immunization workers pointed U.S. forces toward the house in Pakistan where Osama bin Laden was living, which led to his death. Against such a charged backdrop, the power of employing respected community voices cannot be overstated.

Another manifestation of increased voice and agency among communities in global activism is "human-centered design"—a term more often heard in tech innovation. In the context of development, it means a person-centered approach (or for health efforts, "patient-centered"). If you're an activist trying to assist frontline health workers in rural Africa, you need to go there, watch them serve their villages, and engage them directly in the development or design of a new product or system, rather than looking to researchers at Stanford or Oxford for ideas. Trust that communities know what they need and what will work. Then develop your intervention with those perspectives in mind. Allow the health workers to test it, and take their responses to heart.

Human-centered design has improved and accelerated products developed for both commercial and social purposes—sometimes both at the same time. For example, d.light, a company founded in 2006 by two social entrepreneurs, Sam Goldman and Ned Tozun, who wanted to bring safe, bright, nonpolluting light to people around the globe. Sam was driven, in part, by his experience as a Peace Corps volunteer in rural Benin, where he'd been badly burned by a kerosene lamp. Ned had experience in human-centered design. Their idea was to create a solar-powered lantern. For more than a decade, the pair revised multiple prototypes based on feedback from users, eventually joining with social design firm IDEO.org. Since then, d.light has expanded to offer solar energy solutions for homes and small businesses across the globe, selling more than 220 million solar lights and power products in some 70 countries. Beyond their millions of customers, d.light calculates that their products have offset 23 million tons of carbon.

Here's another example, from my days with PATH, when we were trying to address one of the leading causes of maternal mortality: post-partum bleeding after childbirth. In more affluent communities, where women deliver in clinics or hospitals, there is a ready set of interventions for bleeding—drugs, tools, surgery. But poor societies, with at-home births attended by neighbors or midwives, have few such supplies. When a woman starts to bleed, front-line workers make do with whatever they have on hand, often jerry-rigging a condom by filling it with water and inserting it into the uterus to stanch the bleeding until a woman can get to the hospital. At PATH, we were intrigued by this locally conceived solution and wanted to help improve it. So our teams accompanied rural midwives for months, observing their challenges. Then, working with them, PATH developed a hygienic and reusable uterine balloon tamponade, adapted from the condom idea. That design, endorsed by the midwives with further input from gynecologists and medical-device specialists, was eventually produced at commercial scale. It is now manufactured and distributed by a South African company—a low-cost, lifesaving tool that came from the community, for the community.

Extending this person-centered emphasis all the way to its logical end means empowering individuals to take control of their own well-being, literally handing people the tools to take care of themselves. A program called GiveDirectly does exactly that, believing that "people living in poverty deserve the dignity to choose for themselves how best to improve their lives." Through its website, GiveDirectly donors can send money straight to Africans in need, rather than relying on aid organizations to decide how those funds should be spent. Since its founding in 2009, GiveDirectly reports that it has disbursed $140 million in cash to 130,000 families, who've used the money to buy medicine, pay school fees, and purchase farm animals, water, and vehicles. It's another version of the same undercurrent, an approach to development that moves us away from paternalistic models and gives individuals more agency to make choices for their lives.

The health-sector corollary is self-care—that is, putting medical devices directly in the hands of people who need them, instead of requiring that they visit a clinic. This has been the norm for decades, of course, through home testing for pregnancy and other diagnostics. But now in rural Africa, women can self-inject long-lasting contraceptives—an absolute game-changer in family planning that, in turn, allows the children they choose to bear more food, care, and opportunities for a healthier life.

Even at the highest levels, I see a distinct shift toward giving communities more say in the ways we help them address challenges. The Global Fund for Tuberculosis, AIDS and Malaria, for instance, distributes billions of dollars from Geneva but leaves the design for spreading that aid to country-level committees. The World Bank's Global Financing Facility for Women, Children and Adolescents and the recently-launched China International Development Cooperation Agency are both structured around *countries* initiating proposals, in contrast to USAID and bilateral government donors that develop programs centrally and bid out their execution. Ethiopia and India now frequently dictate the conditions of development programs, to the point where they often determine which partners may be selected by foreign donors to work in their countries. From Washington, DC, to London, Geneva, and beyond, this undercurrent of community-centered development means that the job of aid administrators, philanthropic program officers, and international relief and development organizations will change dramatically.

After observing this transition toward community-oriented development, it struck me as parallel to trends I recognized in business—along the lines of Amazon's obsession with "delighting" its users. A customer-centered approach has been standard in most multinational corporations, consulting firms, and small businesses for years. But in the social sector, not so much. Probably because it forces some difficult questions: What is our real purpose? Who is our true client? How should our value be measured and by whom?

Shortly after arriving at PATH, I tried to float this business-influenced concept.

"Let's call it 'the country-as-customer,'" I proposed to my executive team, as we prepared to share the new strategy.

It did not go over well. Some cringed at the commercial overtones. *We're not selling anything. We have a higher mission. We trying to help people*, they said. Others felt I was talking straight from McKinsey's consultant-speak playbook. A few worried that the title would offend major donors and partners, like the Gates Foundation and USAID, who considered themselves our clients. And more than one informed me that I was simply incorrect; by their logic the true customer in philanthropy was always the donor, and our job was to keep donors happy in order to get the next grant.

Nothing in this new strategy was as controversial as identifying countries, rather than people, as the true focus of our work. But the ailing child on a dusty street was rarely PATH's direct customer. We served her by working with the government systems shaping her life and those of the people in her community. Our approach usually targeted public health infrastructure—meaning national and regional governments were our true clients. We were the social-sector equivalent of a business-to-business enterprise.

This proved to be a confusing concept. But we pressed ahead, focusing on the value proposition for any new project under consideration: Was the community demanding our work, and would our presence add anything lasting? For every technology or service we planned to develop, we analyzed how would it be used, the anticipated economic impact, and whether it was actually needed. We formalized things that may sound painfully obvious: listening, understanding, and being part of a community in order to better answer its health challenges.

To make these changes at scale, we needed to establish a new style of leadership in many of our country offices. We steered away from managers who saw themselves as program implementers working on behalf of donors, instead hiring people more closely tied to local communities. These new country directors would serve as relationship builders and ambassadors, business developers, and solution providers. When devising healthcare innovations, we aimed at locales where they might have the greatest impact, so that local governments could then scale up our interventions to serve all citizens. If a health minister, local business, or community-based organization needed assistance around advancing health, we hoped that PATH would be their first call.

We also started thinking of our donors as partners, rather than clients. Our success would be judged through a country's health outcomes, rather than the volume of grants in our pipeline. I'll admit, there was resistance, and we stumbled many times in managing the change. But I believe it put PATH in a better position to catch the momentum of this powerful community-based undercurrent.

In the United States, this move toward community-driven reform is everywhere, spurring advances on everything from immigration policy to education. It is particularly evident around climate change. In response, perhaps, to environmental regulations being rolled back at the federal level, more than 450 U.S. cities now have passed their own commitments to reduce carbon emissions.

In Seattle, frustration with the region's worsening social problems and infrastructure challenges during a period of booming economic growth inspired a group of 19 CEOs from major businesses and global organizations to try working together on solutions. Called Challenge Seattle, these leaders from Microsoft, Starbucks, Boeing, Expedia, the Gates Foundation, PATH, and others form a decidedly pro-business caucus. But our common aim is improved livability for the region—an essential underpinning for continued economic growth. Through its network of partners, Challenge Seattle is helping tackle the city's shortage of housing, its congested transit, and unequal public schools. It has helped shape a more integrated approach to economic development for our multi-county region, supported the design and funding of a large middle-class housing initiative, and initiated large commitments by companies to reduce single-occupancy commuter vehicles region-wide. Challenge Seattle is an intensely local model—despite the global heft of its membership—and presents an inspiring opportunity for community-based change.

During the COVID-19 pandemic, I was on the phone with members of this group nearly every day. Even as the WHO and national governments worldwide issued health directives on best practices for mitigating the global pandemic, it played out as a hyper-local event. Seattle, as it turned out, was one of the first U.S. epicenters, and through Challenge Seattle we had an unusually robust framework for coordinating a regional response. Daily, our members discussed ways to get the word out about "social distancing," confront supply-chain issues, and mitigate adverse economic impacts. That community-based scaffolding, built five years before, served us well in a crisis. As masks and respirators ran short, we were able to fan out and contact entrepreneurs who were designing alternatives. From this vantage point, I could not miss the importance of local context and how differently communities worldwide handled the challenge. One of the most positive, lasting legacies of the tragic epidemic is surely its reminder of the power in local volunteerism, activism, and leadership.

Of course, it doesn't take a pandemic to reveal the power of community-centered activism in addressing social problems. I think of my own hometown in Montana, and the many ways it represents the ideal of rural communities where people take care of each other through thick and thin. So it has been jarring, during recent trips home to Dillon, to see graphic billboards and tough-minded articles filling local newspapers about the horrific toll of methamphetamines and opioid addiction on my childhood community. It's true in Dillon and virtually every other part of rural America. One of the worst ripples is the effect on children of addicted parents. Between 2009 and 2015, child neglect cases spiked 130 percent in Montana, and by 2019, nearly 4,000 children had been taken into foster care. Nine years before, Montana had just 230 kids in care.

But Montana's overdose rates are trending downward, currently at about half the national average. Doctors are writing fewer prescriptions for opioid-based pain relief, which may have helped. There is also wider availability of the anti-overdose medication naloxone, more local education and medication-assisted treatment programs, and most notably a large increase in number of frontline counselors.

While federal and state funding for anti-addiction efforts helps, the nuts and bolts of Montana's response was driven by communities. No surprise, as the many causes of addiction—mental health challenges, financial desperation, dependency on pain medication—cry out for tailored interventions. In one community after another, nurses and other caregivers say the same thing: addiction treatment works best with an extremely high-touch, patient-centered approach. Building treatment approaches around each patient's particular circumstances and needs—without judgment—appears to offer the most promising results. In two Washington State counties, jails have become de facto treatment centers, administering the anti-addiction medication Suboxone to inmates with opioid dependencies. The same is true in parts of Maryland, Massachusetts, and California. In each case, the marked decrease in recidivism through this public health–style approach has been encouraging enough to impress law enforcement.

I recently had dinner with a ski guide who also worked as a nurse in a nearby rural mountain town. She described the catastrophic toll that opioid addiction was leveling on her community and its health system. Solving this riddle is now her full-time job.

"It all starts with the patient," she said. "Everyone is so different, in what they need, in the reasons they are there, in their approach to treatment."

"Yes," I said. "I see that so often in public health. One-size-fits-all rarely works."

"For sure. We're not just treating these folks medically, but trying to address the reasons they found themselves in this situation in the first place," she said. "Each community—and each person—brings different circumstances and support systems, so we have to adjust our approach to match."

I wondered if my nurse friend was merely acting the good soldier, repeating what she'd been trained to believe. So, thinking about the evolving trend toward community-centered approaches, I pressed a bit harder.

"Does this idea of fine-tuning your approach for each patient really come from the community, or are you being told to implement yet another new program developed by someone else, far away?"

She responded with the same steely calm I'd seen earlier that day as we skied a sheer cliff covered in deep powder snow. "I can assure you, I would not be doing this work unless we were permitted to shape the approach ourselves. These are our friends, families, neighbors. We know what they are experiencing—and hopefully, what they need. It wouldn't work any other way."

In such conversations, I think back to the lessons from TB control in Mumbai—building partnerships and programs focused on the patient and community. We conceived our game plan by focusing on the particulars of the community before us, being realistic about its customs and needs. We adapted our model to the habits of the people we wanted to serve—both the patients and private practitioners—rather than attempting to force behavior change. The solution to an enormous public health problem, we found, required working *with* the community, rather than *on* it. Or from the community's perspective, "nothing about us without us."

What does a community-centered mindset mean for practical activists? A lot more listening. We need to hear from communities about how they feel, what they need, and what they want to do themselves. We must understand *how* they want to be helped and then conceive solutions with the patient or farmer or student at the forefront of our thinking. We need to support communities in building their own capacities, providing assistance as needed, rather than going in to do the work ourselves. We need to look for models that support the development of community voice as a foundational principle. Ultimately, we must support and serve the leaders and decisions of the community.

Easier said than done, of course. Each of these approaches means ceding control to some extent—trusting that people know what to do to take care of themselves—even as we provide financial aid. It is true that the global north still invents many of the "answers" and sends them to the global south. But in 2020, there are innovators worldwide, and they need resources to develop and distribute their ideas. Practical activists must be alert to these opportunities for reversing the traditional flow of innovation.

Realizing this trend will not be easy. I expect a long journey with many hurdles. Imagining a world where practical activism is truly community-centered requires a dramatic leap of faith, and it means big changes on many fronts—from rebalancing power relationships to navigating cultural barriers to reconceiving models for accountability. Certainly, there will always be circumstances that demand a more top-down, supply-side strategy—for instance, during epidemic outbreaks, natural disasters, or violent conflicts. In such situations, we'll need to mobilize a large humanitarian response, usually from outside. And some tools, like vaccines, are global in nature, so we should maintain global mechanisms for developing, approving, and purchasing them. Political and financial conditions associated with such aid and development programs will naturally preserve vestiges of the old-school model.

But when trying to solve the world's largest problems, giving communities the tools and authority to shape their own destinies will be transformative. It doesn't take much convincing when you've had the chance to sit in a large room watching young African leaders work together on building a new information exchange for continent-wide medical systems, as I did not long ago in Arusha, Tanzania. Frankly, it was thrilling. To see the people in this group—with their extraordinary passion, digital sophistication, collaborative spirit, and drive for leadership—taking the reins to improve outcomes for their communities was a testament to the horizon ahead.

I believe so strongly in this new approach to activism that I wear a reminder of its power every day. I received it in the DRC, during the summer of 2016, after walking the red-light districts of Lubumbashi, a large, noisy city near the Zambian border. I was utterly out of place there, a white guy in a blazer, with minimal French, being escorted by community workers through streets lined with beer stands, dance clubs, and food vendors—motorcycles, revelers, and sex workers everywhere. In the midst of this mayhem, PATH had set up mobile HIV testing units in a few vacant lots, and the community workers, whom we'd designated as "HIV champions," were encouraging bar patrons to come inside our mobile clinics for screening.

It went on for hours until, well past midnight, I found myself in a dingy cafeteria sitting with eight guys—most of them sex workers, all of them men who had sex with other men. (The term "gay" is not commonly used in the DRC, since it can be a death sentence.) They were HIV positive, ostracized and rejected by their families. The bonds between them were obvious, but they were cautious with me. I knew they faced unbearable challenges—so poor and cast out that they had to rely on sex work for survival, which exposed them daily to violence, isolation, discrimination, and now this horrible disease.

Yet they were working to educate their peers, doing whatever they could to stem HIV while supporting one another. The whole point of our work there was connecting with communities on the ground, and these activists in Lubumbashi provided an essential link, reaching populations we might never be able to test, treat, or educate otherwise.

"Why did you decide to become HIV champions?" I asked through a translator.

"We have to take care of each other," one striking young man responded quietly. He couldn't have been older than 18 but had clearly lived a hard life. "We are always being attacked, so we are always watching out."

"And what about HIV—can you protect yourselves from it?"

"Yes," replied another. "We can insist on condoms and safe sex. That was very hard to do at first. But we have learned to push back, and now more clients understand the risk."

"We want to tell others about what's safe, and help get them tested," said the man to my left, almost spilling his soft drink in the excitement to explain.

"And is there a gay community here in Lubumbashi?" I asked. I knew this was pushing it, since homosexuality is not a topic one can breach comfortably in African communities, particularly with government officials milling around.

There was a long moment of silence.

"You know, I am a gay man," I said. "I've lived with a man, my husband, for many years, and we've lost friends to AIDS. So I am very proud of what you are doing."

The table fell silent again. The men were stunned. They had never known an authority figure or senior official willing to admit homosexuality.

"What is it like to be gay where you live?" asked the youngest man.

We talked into the night. I told them about my family, about coming out, and how, while my life was nothing like theirs, I understood something of their struggle.

In the early morning as we departed, each man hugged me, then they presented me with a copper bracelet. I have not taken it off since. It reminds me of the point of this work—helping communities lift themselves to transform lives.

4

Leveling the Field

Activism through the Lens of Equity

Without women's equal access to positions of decision-making power and a clear process to get there, gender equality, global security, and peace will never be realized.

—Winnie Byanyima, executive director, UNAIDS

I OFTEN WONDER why we see billion-dollar commitments to work on eradicating polio, HIV, and intermittent epidemic outbreaks, but nothing comparable for targeting a preventable disease that reliably kills hundreds of thousands of women every single year. We already have the medicines, tools, and protocols to prevent, screen for, and treat this disease. Yet we will allow legions of poor and middle-aged women to die a painful, drawn-out death from cervical cancer this year. It's outrageous.

At least part of the reason is their status. In many communities, women and girls are not allowed to own property, retain employment, or receive government services. By custom, they often are the last to eat dinner, the last to be educated, and the last to be paid for their work. They are almost always the last in line for healthcare.

Gender inequity is deeply embedded in modern life at every level, whether in the rich world or the poor. In global health initiatives, gender bias appears frequently, as many women's issues—including cervical cancer—have not received the attention they deserve. Around the world, women and girls suffer and die disproportionately through female infanticide, genital cutting, early and forced marriage, polygamy, rape, and HIV (where the rate of infection is now higher for women than men). Even something as basic as being young means more death for females (pregnancy complications are the leading cause of death for adolescent girls globally). The same goes for growing old, since elderly women have less access to retirement benefits, healthcare, and social services than men. Even within philanthropies and nonprofits advancing global health—whose very mission is to do good and to right injustice—it rears its ugly head. Look at the mostly male leadership of international aid and development organizations, and it's hard to ignore the possibility of a relationship between these patterns.

You may be tempted to assume that this pattern is a fast-waning part of the past. But you would be wrong. When the United Nations set its Millennium Development Goals in 2000—benchmarks for eight indicators of global well-being to be achieved by 2015—the numbers for maternal mortality consistently fell short of the target. More than 800 women worldwide still die daily from complications due to pregnancy or childbirth—most of them in sub-Saharan Africa and Southern Asia. To be sure, we have made huge strides. During the three decades between 1990 and 2018, maternal deaths decreased by nearly half, and that should be heralded. Loudly. Still, in our lagging progress on reducing women's cancers, postpartum hemorrhage, and other health indicators, the troubling pattern lingers. In every area, from scientific research to executive power to cultural parity, women's well-being suffers. This is systemic bias.

Well into the twenty-first century, with all our innovation and advancement, it is time to ask why we are still so far from balancing power and privilege between the genders. And do something about it.

Imbalances between the status of women and men stretch well beyond health indicators in poor countries. The World Economic Forum projects that, globally, it will take 99 years to achieve parity between the genders in political representation, workplace opportunities, and access to education. (The U.S. rate—151 years—is even worse.) Women are 47 percent more likely to suffer severe injuries in a car crash, likely because seats, seatbelts, and airbags are designed primarily by men, though it's hard to say for sure because no one has bothered to research why. Meanwhile, women will spend a collective 200 million hours today hauling water. And 41,000 girls under 18 will become child brides. Recent findings from the UN Development Program provide a bleak context for those figures: a report issued in 2020 found that in 75 countries comprising the bulk of the world's population, 90 percent of people are biased against women.

These disparities exist even within organizations dedicated to women's well-being. Though women account for three-quarters of health workers, they are rarely the ones making high-level policy decisions. Seventy percent of the world's ministers of health are men. Seventy-six percent of the WHO's executive board are men, and 96 percent of healthcare companies included on the Fortune Global 500 are led by men. At the World Economic Forum in Davos, almost all senior level discussions about healthcare are dominated by men. Pedro Conceição, director of the UN office that developed the social norm index on gender, called the numbers "shocking."

The collective outrage around these trends is growing so loud and so forceful that it is powering an undercurrent that will shape social activism through the next decade and beyond. Though I will focus this chapter primarily on gender, issues around equity include systemic biases involving race, ethnicity, tribes, sexual identity, disabilities, and a range of other communities. The changemakers driving efforts to correct these biases come out of every walk of life—from rural Africa to European royalty—and their focus on redressing unacceptable inequities is creating a tide of change. They are channeling their activism into actionable conversations, research, policies, programs, and movements to level the playing field. As Sheryl WuDunn and Nicholas Kristof put it in their wonderful book, *Half the Sky: Turning Oppression into Opportunity for Women Worldwide*, "In the nineteenth century, the central moral challenge was slavery. In the twentieth century, it was the battle against totalitarianism. We believe that in this century the paramount moral challenge will be the struggle for gender equality around the world."

Discussions around equity are complex and often sensitive. They touch on cultural traditions of imbalance between different religious groups and economic castes. Very often, efforts to address a single injustice sprawl into historic unfairness across multiple categories. Let's look again at cervical cancer. Nearly all of the hundreds of thousands of women who die of that disease each year live in low- to middle-income countries where screening and treatment programs are rare—primarily because the people deciding where to target resources for health haven't chosen to prioritize research, prevention, or treatment of cervical cancer among the poor. But even in the United States, where survival rates are comparatively high, black women die of the disease at twice the rate of whites, often because their cancers are diagnosed later. And when it is finally caught, black women are less likely to receive surgery for it—even when they have health insurance comparable to that of white women.

Look deeper and more inequities arise. The leading cause of cervical cancer is human papillomavirus (HPV), and a vaccine for it has been available for more than a decade. Widely used in middle-income and richer countries, the HPV vaccine has only recently become available in parts of the developing world. But many girls there still aren't getting inoculated, partly because broad-based vaccination campaigns traditionally focus on infants and very young children. Adolescent girls? Not so much. Cultural norms have a powerful effect too. The HPV vaccine is best administered when a girl is 10 or 11 years old—before she becomes sexually active—but in some communities, frank discussion of a disease linked to sexuality is taboo. Then there are supply shortages and the cost of the vaccine, which can vary from $4 to $154. The upshot of all these hurdles? Where global vaccine experts had anticipated that 40 million girls would be inoculated with the HPV vaccine by the end of 2020, forecasts have been radically scaled back, to 14 million.

My aim here is not to unpack the intricacies of cervical cancer prevention, nor to provide insight on the complex underpinnings of gender or other types of inequality. There are far more capable scholars thinking and writing about those things. As a white American male, I am painfully aware of the ways my own history and experience limit a nuanced understanding of these issues, and often find myself confounded about the best ways to use my voice for advancing this work.

But advance it we must.

Equity as a concept has a moral power. But the rightness of leveling the playing field is not the only reason I believe this idea will drive activism forward. Put plainly, a focus on equity actually improves outcomes. When I was the director of social innovation at McKinsey, I frequently met with business tycoons and political leaders in places like Istanbul, Seoul, and Davos. Sometimes they were newly flush billionaires, other times, veteran CEOs. And when they were through talking with our consultants about better ways to do "lean management," they turned toward their legacies. "What is the single most important thing I can do to improve the world?" they would ask me.

It's an overly simplistic question because, of course, it all depends—on the metrics you're using, the political context, the ways in which you judge success. But I never hesitated in my answer: educate girls.

The business leaders were often surprised by my assertion. But they understood numbers, and the data is clear. Worldwide, an estimated 130 million girls between the ages of 6 and 17 do not attend school. The economic hit resulting from their limited lifetime earnings and productivity? Between $15 trillion and $30 trillion, per country, according to a 2018 report issued by the World Bank. Educate girls and they are more likely to get better jobs, which increases household incomes and helps alleviate poverty. They are more likely to marry later, have fewer children, seek medical help for their kids, and care better for their families. Children born to mothers who can read are more likely to survive past age five and to be vaccinated. UNESCO finds that if all mothers had secondary education, child mortality rates would be cut in half. In other words, improving the well-being of women has powerful ripple effects, raising the quality of life for a whole family and, eventually, its descendants.

As a lecturer at Stanford's business school, I am occasionally invited to work on cross-campus initiatives, and recently one of them centered on women in global health. I was supposed to sit on a panel initially to be called "Men Who Get It."

The invitation came from my friend Michele Barry, director of Stanford's Center for Innovation in Global Health. Michele is always thinking about equity in public health, and she has become particularly focused on the need for more women leaders in our field.

Michele had a picture pinned to her office wall that showed WHO Director-General Dr. Tedros discussing global health priorities—which almost always concern women and children—at a table full of men. This kind of imbalance always leaves a bad taste in my mouth, since our very mission is to level the playing field for all people. But I'm not sure any men really "get it." Even the best-intentioned of us are bumbling forward, finding our way. (To his credit, Dr. Tedros has since appointed many women to leadership positions at the WHO.)

Though I'm privileged as an educated white man from a wealthy country, I do have some sense of what it feels like to be systematically excluded. As a gay man, I know what it means to fight for the same rights that others enjoy as a matter of course. Not that long ago, people like me were routinely barred from housing, fired from jobs, denied healthcare, and ousted from military service in the United States. During the 1990s we had to fight just to get *The New York Times* to print the word "gay." Nevertheless, despite my personal experience of the ways formalized discrimination can ruin lives, I still flounder on matters of gender equity, and I know it.

This has become especially clear as I meet women activists who are focused not only on addressing gender inequity in the world, but within the field of global development itself. Often, they have been galvanized by the experiences of their own mothers or grandmothers, prohibited from owning property in countries like Nigeria. Abstract notions of fairness and "should" disappear when you meet such activists. In Nigeria, for example, they have fought year after year for passage of a gender equality bill that would outlaw child marriage—so far, defeated by lawmakers who see themselves as safeguarding Nigerian cultural tradition.

Unbowed, this new generation of practical activists is turning toward community conversations, keenly aware that changing laws will mean first changing minds around women's economic empowerment. Blessing Omakwu is a young Nigerian-American lawyer leading this work and simultaneously elevating the voices of African women within the global development conversation. "These voices are the most marginalized in the development dialogue," she told me. "Even in the U.S., you rarely find people of color in development—and only in a support capacity. They're rarely in the room making decisions, certainly not on policy. It's a huge tension in this field. We're not practicing what we preach."

Back at Stanford, Michele appreciated both my experience and awareness of its limitations. That's how I ended up at a conference on women leadership in global health on a renamed panel of men identified as "allies." It was awkward, because I'm hardly a perfect exemplar. Early in my career, I struggled with female bosses—they reminded me of my mother, which was confusing. Later, in management roles, I often failed to appreciate the ways my decisions and biases affected gender imbalances until it was too late. So I talked about our need, as men, to open the door to new kinds of leadership. I won't sugarcoat this: it was difficult to hash through these issues on stage, in public. There I was, leading one of the largest nonprofits in global development, well aware that my gender had given me a disproportionate advantage in getting there. I am one among so many. The recently published Global Health 50/50 Report 2020, introducing a discussion about "decolonializing" global development, finds that more 80 eighty percent of global health leaders are nationals of high-income countries and some 70 percent of CEOs are men (including at PATH). Just 5 percent of the leaders in our sector are women from low- and middle-income countries. Best-scenario forecasts say that at current rates it will take a half-century to reach gender parity in senior management.

Consequences of the imbalance ripple well beyond our boardrooms. Look at data collection. Fewer women are included in scientific research, and results often are not disaggregated by gender—meaning that doctors make treatment decisions for women based on research that is valid primarily for men (more specifically, white men of wealthier nations whose diet and lifestyles may further skew the results). Meanwhile, women's diseases tend to receive less funding for study, and in most scientific fields, men get bigger research grants. A growing body of evidence suggests that studies led by men are assumed to be more credible than those headed by women. "We find a startling mismatch between global burdens of disease and the stated priorities of global health organizations and funders," the Global Health 50/50 Report bluntly notes. It also states that so-called gender-blindness only perpetuates health inequities further, resulting in more "people being denied their right to the highest attainable standard of health and well-being." In short, we need a lot more women in our executive suites—not just because it's the right thing to do, but because taking a stronger gender-oriented approach is the single most powerful tool we have to improve equity and human well-being on a global scale.

A word here about the terms *equity* and *equality*. They are not interchangeable. Equality, as its root suggests, means treating all people the same. That's fine when everyone starts from the same place. But we don't. Equity, in contrast, means providing what each group needs to be successful. For those starting at the back of the line, that will mean getting a bigger boost—a distinctly not-equal response. Educators illustrate this concept very effectively with a picture showing three children of different heights, each trying to see over a fence. The tallest child already has a clear view. The middle-sized child may need only a short stepstool. But the smallest child will need a big leg up just to get to the same level as the other two and see the same view. That's equity. It necessarily involves giving more to some over others, so discussions about equity often raise hackles among people who are more comfortable talking about equality (which would mean tearing down the fence altogether).

These differences are not semantic. Equity focuses less on morality than on addressing the underlying systems that keep those at the back of the line from ever catching up. Here's an example: in almost all countries, women live longer than men. This is inherently unequal, but it's due mainly to biology. On the other hand, when Indian women die of preventable diseases due to disparities in nutrition at rates far exceeding those for Indian men, that's a matter of equity, and it needs to be addressed.

This commitment requires new policies and approaches across the board, including in global health. Gavi, the vaccine alliance, demonstrated an understanding of this from the start. Credited with saving some 13 million lives since 2000, Gavi is often highlighted as a recent success story in global health. Nonetheless, the group has fallen short of some of its goals. Its leaders had deemed the years between 2010 and 2020 the "Decade of Vaccines." But they faced problems around the introduction of new drugs, logistical hurdles reaching remote communities, and pushback from the anti-vaccine movement. It would have been easier, surely, to focus on overall coverage—boosting their global numbers. But when adopting a new strategy in 2019, the Gavi board explicitly decided to focus instead on equity and "leave no one behind." That is, their aim was ensuring that more vaccines went to the hardest-to-reach patients, emphasizing outreach to women and children who live in remote areas, or as refugees, or within patriarchal communities that made them particularly difficult to serve. That's practical activism through an equity lens.

In the social sector, an emphasis on equity, diversity, and inclusion parallels our overall goals. But that focus correlates to better outcomes in many other industries too, particularly those powered by innovation, creativity, and person-to-person contact. A recent study in the *Harvard Business Review* analyzed data from 1,069 of the planet's leading companies and found that in places like Scandinavia, where gender parity is a cultural value, diverse businesses posted better numbers—higher market value, revenues, and productivity.

One of the main reasons that diversity often correlates to an organization's success is its improved alignment with customer needs. In other words, elevating the voices and experiences of people who more closely represent those you're trying to reach is going to help you serve them better. We saw evidence of this in Vietnam's successful Healthy Markets program to fight HIV/AIDS, which focused on and was piloted by gay men, a market that had traditionally lacked access to such targeted services. The anti-TB program in Mumbai similarly incorporated the values and traditions of slum-dwellers by hiring field workers from that community who provided an essential link to the network of informal caregivers with whom PATH needed to connect. "A gender equal world would be wealthier, healthier, more peaceful, and more equitable," Katja Iversen, president of the global advocacy group Women Deliver, reminded the Davos crowd in 2020.

Practical activists consistently need to view their work through this equity lens. But why is it such a big deal now? Haven't activists been fighting for ages to see more fairness and inclusivity? Well, yes. But powerful new forces are at work today. Attention to gender equality, particularly around pay, has sparked growing media attention, legislation, and initiatives. Racial and gender equity, diversity, and inclusion are now top priorities for executives at most major companies and social sector organizations. The "Me Too" movement in particular has focused the world on the prevalence of workplace behavior—often unlawful—that keeps women down. The social sector has not been immune. Disturbing sexual harassment events that have come to light at Oxfam, Mercy Corps, and The Nature Conservancy have led to painful self-reflection and leadership changes. As a result, the entire sector is undertaking some hard self-study.

Outrage is not the only reason behind this strengthening undercurrent. Gender equality is enshrined in the UN's Sustainable Development Goals for 2030 (SDG 5), though most countries are still far from meeting the targets. And influencers around the globe are embracing it. From Melinda Gates's powerful book *The Moment of Lift* to the inclusive agenda promoted by political leaders like Canadian prime minister Justin Trudeau, gender equality is at the top of the world agenda. Michelle Obama launched the Girls Opportunity Alliance to work on girls' education. Princess Mabel van Oranje-Nassau of the Netherlands founded Girls Not Brides to focus attention on ending child marriage. And Nobel Peace Prize winner Malala Yousafzai of Pakistan founded a charity dedicated to making sure every girl on the planet can receive a free, safe, quality education. Twenty-five years after the Beijing Declaration on the role of women, we see enormous strides in every area, from women's health to women's education and political empowerment. In his book *Factfulness*, Hans Rosling makes this very point, noting that while stark gender injustice persists, huge progress has been made. More women have more rights, young girls attend primary school at rates nearly equal to those of young boys, and each of these efforts has built on the previous. "What is happening today is the culmination of all the waves of women's efforts that went before," Canadian human rights activist Sally Armstrong wrote in *The Unfinished Business of Girls' Rights*. "Once change like this begins in earnest, once it has lifted off, the momentum picks up and it becomes unstoppable."

You could be forgiven for skepticism, however. In some parts of the world, momentum toward gender equality, and equity in general, has spurred a vicious backlash. Racial division and inequity in many communities is more acute than ever. Religious turmoil and tribal conflicts continue to flame. Hostility toward LGBTQI people is increasing in certain countries, and blatant misogyny has resulted in some regressive new policies. These data points are disheartening. But I see them as part of the long, jagged path walked by every social justice movement. The road has never been linear.

What do these competing forces mean for the next generation of activists? Primarily, that every aspect of global development will be viewed through an equity lens—around gender, race, ethnicity, sexuality, and disability. This will show up in tactical ways, such as ensuring balanced and inclusive boards, teams, leadership groups, and career advancement paths. It will show up through new voices at the table when decisions are made. And it will require taking an intentionally gender-specific approach when we design policies and programs.

The equity undercurrent will propel changes in our thinking as well. We'll see data disaggregated for gender, teasing out important trends that get buried when we view everything through the prism of averages. Because so many programs lack disaggregated data, we have little idea what is really happening with our interventions as they affect women. But what if we reframed our protocols around data collection and analysis to focus on metrics for women and girls rather than overall populations? What if we disaggregated the results to understand not only outcomes by gender, but also how services are accessed by women and girls—or not?

I expect that we'll see an increasing emphasis on combatting diseases like cervical and breast cancer, and more meaningful interventions on health challenges like postpartum hemorrhage. The equity undercurrent will reshape designs for community programming in all countries and at every income level. In some places, that will mean doubling down on girl's education, or fighting cultural practices that require menstruating women to sequester themselves because they are considered "impure." In others, it will mean ensuring that women have a place in every profession and at the boardroom table. I'm talking about a groundswell, and I don't see it fading away.

Extraordinary gender-specific programming is already at work across many countries and sectors. In India, China, Myanmar, and parts of Africa, the nonprofit Landesa is working to change inheritance laws because many women—like the activists in Nigeria—do not have the right to own property (though they are often the ones working the land). Over the past decade, the global humanitarian agency CARE has boosted its research and programming around gender-based violence, child marriage, dignified work, girl's education, and sexual and reproductive health. Microfinance organizations are targeting loans and technical assistance to female entrepreneurs in agriculture. (Research shows that a family can raise itself from poverty with as little as a tenth of an acre.) And around the world, community-based organizations are increasingly being formed and led by women to lift up girls with an array of services that challenge traditional norms.

Global Partnerships, a social investment organization that uses microfinance as a platform for improving lives in Latin America and East Africa, assesses its investment portfolio through a gender lens. This is downright revolutionary because, in many countries, women don't have the necessary collateral to secure a loan. In some cases, the barriers may be even more basic—like lacking the time or transportation to get to a bank. If she can get there, a woman may be put off by her treatment, unaware of her options, or thrown by the unfamiliar documentation process. Even when, officially, there is access, women remain excluded.

But in the past 20 years, microfinance has helped women make great strides toward financial self-sufficiency—often by leveraging communal traditions. The idea of lending to groups of women acting as one borrower came when loan officers observed the ways women in a village routinely combined their individual resources for the greater good. With each woman essentially underwriting the credit of another, the social fabric of the group acts as a guarantor to discourage loan delinquency. Over time, as community-focused microcredit institutions established trusting relationships within a village, they became aware of other needs among their female clients—health services, education, business training—and they began to provide those things too.

A pioneer in this all-services approach is the development and microfinance institution Pro Mujer, which works with low-income women in Bolivia, Mexico, Nicaragua, and Peru. Its credit officers are cross-trained to provide preventive health education and screening for chronic diseases during group meetings for loan repayment. In this way, they reach clients and "patients" simultaneously, while keeping costs down. In one of these financially rooted health sessions, women might get education on breast and cervical cancer, diabetes, hypertension, and depression. They might be screened for conditions like diabetes and high blood pressure—all while amassing capital to lift themselves out of poverty. This is what I mean by practical activism through a gender lens.

In Myanmar, where migrant women from rural villages come into the capital city of Yangon for factory work, they are educated on everything from budgeting to nutrition, child-rearing, and reproductive health through a program called Sunday Café. Most participants are young—between the ages of 16 and 25—and they are easy targets for exploitation and abuse. Sunday Café, which receives funding through the social enterprise organization Business Kind, is also supported by factory owners because it builds skills, confidence, opportunity, and better workers.

You can't talk about gender equality without looking at access to contraceptives, and PATH has been committed to family planning since its founding in the 1970s. One of the most exciting projects I watched during my eight years there was the introduction of a long-lasting, injectable contraceptive that women can administer to themselves. No longer must they seek permission from their partners to visit a healthcare worker, then trudge to a faraway clinic and wait on line. Sayana Press, as the neat little device is called, is an all-in-one unit containing a premeasured dose of contraceptive enclosed in a plastic bubble attached to a small needle. One dose lasts three months, the whole thing fits in the palm of your hand, and it's easily storable, a great example of human-centered design. Since Sayana's introduction in 2014, it has been approved for use in more than 60 countries. In Uganda, a third of the women who injected it in 2018 were using family planning for the first time.

Of course, opening the door to more agency and autonomy for marginalized people will eventually lead to harder conversations—for example, around the use of quotas in hiring and governance, approaches to halt culturally sanctioned violence against women, and the tension between religious freedom and individual human rights. It will force an assessment of deeply embedded power structures. It will push the global development agenda toward a focus on underlying determinants; rather than serving victims of discrimination, for instance, global development work with an equity lens could mean rooting out structures that protect the status quo. Have no illusions: this undercurrent is going to cause disruption. As the doctor Paul Farmer says in Tracy Kidder's book *Mountains Beyond Mountains*, "The essence of global health equity is the idea that something so precious as health might be viewed as a right."

Like every undercurrent outlined in this book, the momentum I see around equity gives me tremendous hope. Returning to cervical cancer, more than 100 countries now have the HPV vaccine. That's an increase of almost 30 percent since 2018. Uganda is among the most recent to join the list, and the importance of this became clear to me when I met a middle-aged woman at a clinic there, in the city of Kampala. Too old for the vaccine, she had traveled 8 hours just to be screened for cervical cancer. But innovation was still making a difference in her life, enabling test results while she waited, instead of forcing her to endure another 16 hours of travel home and back. The next generation might not need to make that trip at all. In 2015, the Ugandan cabinet approved a nationwide HPV-immunization program while researchers are busy developing a next-generation vaccine that will provide full protection in a single shot, rather than the current two-dose protocol.

In the meantime, activists are working on programs to treat mothers for cervical cancer when they bring their daughters to get immunized. And scientists are designing AI-enabled diagnostic apps for screening middle-aged women in low-resource settings. Still, old mindsets are tough to break. After finally approving Uganda's national HPV immunization program, one health official there remarked to me, "okay, now you've got to come up with a prostate cancer vaccine for us men."

I am frequently reminded of the jagged path walked in every march toward social justice. In September 2018, my husband Bob and I were invited to one of the first official meetings of the United

Nations General Assembly dedicated to LGBTQI rights. Our community routinely endures horrific violence in countries around the world, as indicated through the story of those HIV champions in Chapter 3. Even with increased legal protection for jobs, housing, and same-sex unions, social ills affect gays and lesbians at strikingly disproportionate rates. In the United States, gay teenagers are four times more likely than straights to attempt suicide. In 29 states it is still legal to fire or evict gay people because of their sexual identity. Happens all the time. Beyond U.S. borders, the situation can be far more dire. In 70 countries, gay relationships are illegal, and consenting adults are routinely imprisoned, harassed, and sometimes thrown off roofs (this happened in Syria). In 13 countries, gay people can be legally put to death. My husband, Bob, has taken a special interest in fighting for gay rights, helping to organize a stunning photography exhibition by *National Geographic* photographer Robin Hammond called "Where Love Is Illegal." These lush, sometimes disturbing images of LGBTQI individuals and couples who've faced discrimination, harassment, violence, or death in Nigeria, Nicaragua, Syria, and the United States tell a powerful story. In September 2018, they were on display at one of the first official meetings of the United Nations General Assembly dedicated to LGBTQI rights, which Bob and I were invited to attend. While each image showed a person whose voice and freedom had been smothered, to see all of them hanging on the walls of the UN—a place committed to a more just and peaceful world—gave both of us a measure of courage.

So many communities are walking the path to justice and equality, and it is often rocky. Still, the overall trendline should provide hope. Kenya exemplifies this duality. Despite that country's rapidly growing economy and increasingly cosmopolitan population, guess which segment has the highest rate of HIV: women. Sixty-seven percent of new HIV cases in sub-Saharan Africa afflict young women and girls. That frightening pattern was much on my mind when I visited the Mama Sisi Safe Space in a densely packed, devastatingly poor neighborhood of Kisumu. Inside its rusted front gates, however, I felt as if I'd entered an oasis. Concern about HIV trends in young women had prompted several major funders to create something called the DREAMS (Determined, Resilient, Empowered, AIDS-free, Mentored, and Safe) partnership. The idea was to confront simultaneously the multiple factors that leave girls vulnerable to HIV: exclusion from economic opportunity, lack of access to secondary school, and gender-based violence. Mama Sisi Safe Space was one of these projects.

Standing in its small courtyard, which served as a shelter, community center, and classroom, I was not treated as the privileged head of a large multinational organization. Instead, I was directed to sign a consent form committing to the rules of the Mama Sisi community, and for the next hour I was mostly silent, listening to a dozen adolescent girls. One by one, each shared her story—of escaping commercial sex work or finding a community to shield her from harassment. Some had known nothing about how to protect themselves from HIV before landing here. Many described the thrill of acquiring marketable skills and, for the first time, feeling empowered, celebrated—even loved. I asked the expected questions: What kinds of programs are you offering these girls? How do you measure your success? What are the biggest challenges you face? What can I do to help you do more?

"We want you to tell others about us," said one of the more outspoken teenagers, "but we don't really need help."

"What is it that you want me to tell them?"

"That we are taking care of each other, and we're going to be okay. Before, we were nothing but girls in the streets. Men took advantage of us all the time. But now we have each other, and we don't need them."

Her pride was clear. But I still didn't understand what precisely had made this place so special. "For the first time, I feel like I am in control of my life," she said when I pressed. "Women and girls need to be treated equally. But we also need to be understood for what our lives are really like, and who we want to become."

As far as I'm concerned, this teenage girl has thrown down a gauntlet for us all.

Digital Disruption

How Activists Must Harness New Technologies to Change the World

Some pessimists warn that technology will usher in a dystopian future. Some naïve optimists predict it will create a utopia. The truth lies somewhere in between. Technology is disruptive, and countries need to invest to maximize the positive disruptions and manage the negative ones.
Bill & Melinda Gates, Goalkeepers Report 2019

PICTURE A SMALL OFFICE, about the size of a portable classroom, filled with a long, metal table holding about 10 computers. The walls are lined with small monitors, each displaying data about a disease outbreak trickling in from across an entire country—like a war room, but for combating disease outbreaks. It's not quite what you'd see in a Hollywood movie, but it's still impressive. Some of the monitors flash with population analyses and raw data on numbers of cases. Others use geomapping to forecast the next likely hotspots. Another set analyzes health worker interventions. More dazzling even than the technology is its location, in Kinshasa, capital city of the Democratic Republic of Congo (DRC), one of the poorest countries on the planet.

The year was 2019, and I was visiting the DRC's Global Health Security Emergency Operations Center, mission control for confronting Ebola virus. In a year, the country would discharge one of its last Ebola patients from treatment, cautiously hopeful that the deadly outbreak had been quashed. But at the time, the DRC and its health minister were in the thick of their tenth virulent bout, trying to get ahead of a virus that would claim more than 2,000 lives in 18 months.

The disease-tracking nerve center where I stood was particularly satisfying to see, as it was the realization of a commitment I'd made to the Minister of Public Health, Dr. Oly Kalenga, several years earlier. He'd struck me as a talented and committed physician. Originally from eastern DRC, Dr. Kalenga had studied epidemiology, public health, and economics in Belgium, but returned home in 2016 to undertake a near-impossible task: transforming the health system of a country decimated by decades of war. Where do you even begin a job like that? Aside from Ebola, Dr. Kalenga had a frightening array of everyday health crises to tackle—maternal death, outbreaks of measles and cholera, vaccination challenges, and HIV and TB control.

Plenty of officials would have considered the pursuit of a digital operations center in DRC ridiculously unrealistic. Two-thirds of the country had no electricity, many roads were impassable, and the government was regarded as one of the most unstable and corrupt on earth. But Dr. Kalenga embraced the job. And his number one aim was finding a way to coordinate and track responses to DRC's numerous health problems. He wanted to collect health data remotely and use analytics to devise targeted, efficient solutions.

People thought he was crazy to talk about digital tools—after all, DRC had so many immediately pressing needs. But Dr. Kalenga was convinced that the right digital strategy could help them jump ahead—even before the country had rebuilt its hospitals and roads.

It's a concept known as "leapfrogging," which means skipping over customary development stages—stringing telephone wire, for example—and hopping straight to mobile technology by building cell phone towers.

Dr. Kalenga believed that with the right digital health tools and data, DRC could leap ahead. He didn't want to wait for the establishment of land lines that might never be completed. He considered geospatial mapping to be a much better way for pinpointing people's locations. He also recognized that it would be a long time before DRC had enough nurses and hospitals for in-person visits, so establishing tools for remote diagnosis seemed, if anything, the most reality-based approach to the problem.

Clearly, he had a vision. What he needed was a team that understood the possibilities and could help him shape his strategy.

To me, the potential upside looked enormous. But back in Seattle, determined to raise money for a digital health strategist in the DRC, we discovered that most donors thought this idea was crazy. The DRC was far too undeveloped to support such a sophisticated operation, they said. Who would use all that high-tech software when the basic system for primary care was so broken? To them, it seemed absurd to envision a digital future there. But the PATH team was persistent. The opportunity to accelerate improved human health through smart tools was tantalizing to them. What if DRC health authorities could begin tracking cases of polio, HIV, and TB through digital surveillance? Could mapping and AI allow them to detect cholera outbreaks earlier? What if a central health center could send text messages reminding mothers of key stages during pregnancy to visit a clinic for prenatal care? And what if each person eventually had a digitized health history so doctors would know of past illnesses or underlying risk when devising a treatment plan? All of these outcomes would be possible through intelligent use of technology.

We ended up raising money to hire a brilliant man from Mali, Ousmane Ly, who worked closely with the minister to shape the country's first digital health strategy. Then, just as that work was getting under way in August 2018, along came a major outbreak of Ebola, in northeastern Kivu Province. Here it was, an opportunity to deploy the digital approach Dr. Kalenga had envisioned and see how it could be used both in crisis scenarios and the everyday. With support from the U.S. Centers for Disease Control, Ousmane and his team built their Global Health Security Emergency Operations Center in Kinshasa, a war room for disease control.

As the epidemic worsened and spread, Ousmane was able to take his operations center on the road. In a van chock-full of computers performing geospatial data analysis, health workers drove to remote locations to gather information and quickly feed it into analytics tools, racing to develop a targeted response before the disease infected still more people. The information helped Ousmane and others figure out where a new vaccine against Ebola would offer the biggest impact. When Dr. Tedros of the WHO visited the DRC for a personal perspective on the response, data analyzed through the emergency operations center helped provide him with a clearer sense of the country's needs than had ever been available before.

Though Dr. Kalenga, accused of financial mismanagement, has since been replaced as minister, and the WHO continues to classify Ebola as a public health emergency, by spring 2020 there were new treatments under development, a promising vaccine, higher levels of care for patients, and—for nearly three months—no new cases. A handful cropped up just days before Dr. Tedros anticipated announcing an end to the outbreak, but DRC was in a much better position to contain them than it had been before. Many factors contributed to these advances—not least, brave health workers risking their lives to treat communities riven by violence—but the role technology played in this improved response cannot be overstated.

Even as we were hoping to celebrate the end of Ebola, another health crisis of staggering proportions was brewing. The COVID-19 pandemic has severely tested the globe's economic, political, and health systems. It has laid bare our shortcomings and vulnerabilities, with terrifying consequences. During the early weeks of the outbreak, as I spoke round-the-clock with health leaders and public officials to assist in local and global responses, the image that came to my mind most frequently was a five-year-olds' soccer game: the whole field racing to follow the ball wherever it was kicked, then piling on, rugby-style, so chaotically that it took weeks to figure out who had the ball and was in charge.

But the COVID-19 pandemic also revealed the incredible opportunities within reach. I was talking with all these global health experts in my role as co-chair of the WHO Digital Health Advisory Group to hear their ideas about ways that digital technology could help. When histories of this pandemic are written, I expect that COVID-19 will represent a milestone in digital health. Every potential and pitfall within our data arsenal was revealed—from new artificial intelligence algorithms speeding us toward new vaccine candidates, to powerful surveillance tools allowing us to understand the disease's trajectory, to the stunning power of social media to both spread and combat misinformation. Telemedicine, too, had its coming of age through the COVID-19 response, supporting faster diagnosis and treatment while relieving pressure on overtaxed health workers. We surfaced new dashboards and analytic models to help with supply chain management for essential medicines. We used knowledge-sharing platforms as never before to disseminate information across communities. And we deployed a host of new digital tools to support government decision-makers, medical workers, and others at the pandemic's front lines.

I remember a fascinating conference call in mid-March 2020 with a gifted technologist from Estonia working on interoperability standards and hosting hackathons; a dedicated public health expert from New Zealand focusing on better data-sharing models while being quarantined at home; an AI expert from a tech company in

China demonstrating tools that other countries could use to scale up testing; a Kuwaiti doctor putting together a national surveillance dashboard to help his government; a Nigerian health expert sharing telemedicine tools that would support communities; and a British specialist adapting video games and social media models to address mental health during this period of anxiety and isolation. While the context was harrowing, never have I been more honored to be working with such dedicated practical activists around the globe, all of them marshaling the power of this digital-revolution undercurrent to save lives.

Ebola and COVID, a one-two punch of overlapping hazards, brought many lessons to the fore. The most fundamental, however, is that technology is changing the activist's world—even in the most remote, underserved corners of our planet.

People have been collecting information for as long as we've been trying to improve life on earth—that's not new. But what we have at our fingertips today is an opportunity to make that information vastly more meaningful. Across every sector where activists work—from healthcare to education, agriculture, climate change, and financial services—technology is the undercurrent with the potential to drive change faster than anything we've ever seen. It is an absolute game-changer, enabling advances in the fight against poverty that were unimaginable just a few years ago. We've barely scratched the surface of what's possible.

However, that thrilling potential brings with it a minefield of new, very real dangers, among them privacy breaches, disinformation spread through social media to increase political polarization, brain-warping internet addiction, bias embedded in artificial intelligence tools, and a widening divide between the wealthy and everyone else. These are forces that could torpedo our common story into one of true dystopia. But I am an optimist and, on balance, I believe the possibilities for tech-powered social change far outweigh the risks. Either way, our digital revolution is the undercurrent that will have the biggest day-to-day impact on the lives of billions around the globe, and social activists will be constantly walking the tightrope between its risks and rewards.

The transformative effects of digital and data tools are particularly pronounced in healthcare. Whether we're using artificial intelligence to detect cervical cancer better than a doctor's human eye, looking to algorithms for help in developing new drugs, or digitally integrating health records to permit better tracking of children's immunization history, global health is bursting with digital innovations aimed at improved well-being. In poor countries the impact, even during a project's first few years, can be profound. For example, health workers in much of Africa have struggled to navigate multiple databases for the same family. One set of information might record vaccinations; another, nutrition programs; in a third, maternal health stats. It was ridiculously time-consuming for nurses to shuttle between them, and it also allowed more chances for error. But what if these disparate data sets were integrated into a single portfolio that followed each patient? Combining data on nutrition and vaccination, for example, could improve detection of interdependencies, comorbidities, and social determinants. It would help healthcare workers understand people's needs holistically.

A version of that idea is under way through the Better Immunization Data Initiative, which was built on the realization that spotty data on vaccinations in Tanzania and Zambia was resulting in fewer children getting vaccinated and a greater risk of disease. The program evolved out of efforts to combat child and maternal mortality. In Tanzania, many women did not give birth in a hospital, so there were no records for their children. This made it nearly impossible to get an accurate count of who had been vaccinated against which diseases. But we noticed that if an infant lived for more than five days, the mothers would generally bring them into a clinic for a first round of immunization. That was the beginning. We realized that these infant immunizations could serve as a proxy birth registry—essentially a database. And then we wondered, could that ad hoc registry be built into health dossiers for each child?

For decades, nurses like Lucy Sanday had spent hours each week combing through record books, tallying the number of kids due for vaccination. Lucy would then cross-check those numbers with her clinic's stock to ensure that she had enough on hand—all before funneling more than 100 children through her doors at the Kaloleni Urban Health Centre near Arusha, Tanzania. Afterward, Lucy and her team would work nights and weekends to log each vaccination by hand on paper reports delivered monthly to the local health district. Often, this meant literally copying numbers from one notebook into another. Some studies estimate that some health workers in Africa spend up to 50 percent of their time recording data.

It was, at best, inefficient, with a high probability for making mistakes. In one district, health workers discovered that the vaccination records for nearly 500 kids were unaccounted for. Worse, after Lucy sent her data to the district office, she rarely saw it again. Had the clinic processed fewer patients this month than last? Impossible to know. And if so, why the sudden drop-off in kids returning for their scheduled shots? With no feedback, the nurses had no way of analyzing their information, recognizing problems, or making data-based decisions to address them. Esther Lungu, the first lady of Zambia, recognized this issue in endorsing our effort to digitize all this information in her country. "Immunization is not sufficient if we don't know who should receive vaccines, where these children are, and what vaccines they should be getting," she said. "This information matters as much as the vaccines. Data is a critical tool in the health service."

The Better Immunization Data Initiative began in earnest in 2015, with an electronic registry that gave children a barcode attached to their medical history and linked their vaccination schedules to supplies in each clinic, so that Lucy and her staff could stay on top of demand. Now, when children arrive for their shots, Lucy scans their barcode, immediately views their records, and enters the immunizations received that day. She can tell if a child due for shots has not shown up, or if he received a vaccination elsewhere. The system also takes care of those monthly reports that used to occupy so much of Lucy's time, generating them electronically and automatically sending the documents to district headquarters. This has supercharged productivity. Health workers in Tanzania cut their time spent on registration and paperwork updates by almost half, and each clinic saved itself 70 hours per year—eight full workdays—in time spent filing forms.

A dashboard also tracks the performance of nurses in Lucy's clinic compared to others, and links them to their colleagues. After three years, the project had registered nearly 500,000 children in Tanzania, and another 97,000 in Zambia, ensuring regular vaccinations and tracking their overall health. The advancement wasn't about a shiny new app; it came from activists who thought about ways to build on the system at hand in ways that would improve the well-being of entire communities.

Of course, such innovations require digital systems that can "talk" to each other, and to many people that sounds frighteningly sci-fi, raising a host of questions about data privacy. On the other hand, you can see how it would be a huge help to the mother who wants to ensure that her children are both well nourished and vaccinated, without traveling to a half-dozen different providers and explaining her needs to someone new each time. Savvy use of digital technology can allow us, ironically, to be much more responsive to people's real lives.

In a place like the DRC—one of those countries at the very bottom of the diamond, where basic infrastructure has been decimated—improving lives at scale might be impossible without the opportunities afforded through digital technology. For example, health workers there used mapping applications to attack sleeping sickness, a pernicious disease that comes from infected tsetse flies.

If left untreated, it is usually fatal. But sleeping sickness occurs almost exclusively in rural areas of the DRC that are difficult to reach by road and very undeveloped. Using satellite photography, data analysts were able to map all the roofs in one hotspot, then index the size and type of roof to the likely number of family members inside. Those two pieces of data, filtered through a machine-learning algorithm, allowed researchers to identify more than 4,000 remote villages that had never been mapped before and create a baseline number to measure the effects of their effort in eliminating the disease.

A similar idea using different technology helped PATH to dramatically cut malaria rates in Zambia. This awful disease was eliminated from the United States in 1951. But it still kills more than 400,000 people each year, mostly young children in Africa and South Asia. At PATH, we'd vowed to help eliminate it in other countries, so we launched the Visualize No Malaria project. But malaria is particularly difficult to manage because most people who have the mosquito-borne parasites that cause it show no symptoms. The community challenge was to stop the mosquitos that spread these parasites. But first, health workers needed to understand its prevalence in a given community. So, with handheld devices like mobile phones they recorded the visibly sick people. Then, using an algorithm to track mosquito flight patterns, they tested everyone within that catchment area and administered anti-malaria drugs on a mass scale. Via texting technology, they "nudged" patients to follow through with medication, along the same lines as we'd done in India to remind TB patients about completing their full course of treatment. The result of our Visualize No Malaria project? A 95 percent reduction in cases over four years, nearly eliminating of the disease in that province of Zambia.

The same protocol has since been scaled to Senegal, Ethiopia, and 14 other countries. As with the Better Immunization Data Initiative, success on crushing malaria did not hinge on developing any new medication. It intelligently adapted technology we already had.

Powerful data visualization and digital tools also offer communities the chance to leapfrog over slow-developing infrastructure, like roads and telephone lines—just as health officials had envisioned in the DRC. They were thinking about improved communication via cell phones instead of landlines. But the same cellular technology can give kids in underdeveloped nations access to the educational powers of the internet. It doesn't take much imagination to see how this leap might transform more than the health of a community.

After childhood vaccination and maternal health, the bedrock of global development work is education. In the United States, tracking student data has become extremely controversial. But it's difficult to argue with results like those from Khan Academy, which uses machine learning to provide students with increasingly more difficult work, building their skills. Twelve years ago, Salman Khan, a hedge fund analyst in Boston, had no such plans. He was merely tutoring his sixth-grade cousin in math, over the phone. Using an early online platform called Doodle Images, Khan would illustrate the concepts he was trying to explain and send these rudimentary videos to his cousin. Pretty soon, more young relatives began asking for help, along with their friends. To keep up with the growing number of requests, Khan began recording his video tutorials and posting them on YouTube—a website he once considered silly, "something for dogs on skateboards."

Within four years, more than three million schoolchildren were watching. Even Bill Gates's kids were fans. But Khan had grown up poor, and he was particularly interested in bringing math education to parts of the world where school was a barebones affair, with few textbooks or highly trained teachers. His audacious goal: to provide "a free world-class education for anyone, anywhere."

Venture capitalists began to take notice, providing enough seed money for Khan to quit his job as a financier and found Khan Academy. Today, his lessons are available in more than 36 languages, educating some 80 million people. That's digital transformation at scale.

Anyone who has ever perused school testing data knows what a morass it is. The same for health metrics. But better tools help us see the patterns within those myriad data points so we can devise smarter interventions—whether in education, healthcare, financial services, or agriculture.

I am sometimes accused of being a proselytizer for digital technology—amusing, when you consider what a Luddite I used to be. As a religion major at Princeton, I didn't even know where the engineering school was, and I am still often the last person to adopt new digital tools or download the best apps. Even today as a digital health leader, I don't believe that high-performance computing or artificial intelligence holds the answer to all our problems. At Davos one year I sat on a panel called "Health Systems: Leapfrogging in Emerging Economies" and reminded the audience that the foundation of health is still fundamentally a matter of biology and chemistry—it hasn't been overtaken by only bits and bytes. The greatest technology in the world means little without a functioning health system and the right expertise, medicines, and protocols. Still, for social activists I can't think of a force in our world today with greater potential for changing the future of human development than digital technology.

One of the most exciting aspects of my work, whether at PATH, the WHO, or Stanford, has been the access it gives me to test-drive scores of cool new applications and products pitched by students, social entrepreneurs, researchers, companies, and hackers. Whether they are good ideas or not, fundable or destined for the dustbin, the ingenuity, passion, and energy fueling these technologies for social impact fill me with optimism. Beyond innovations in healthcare and education, technology has built pathways for getting micropayments to the bottom end of our global diamond through digital banking that enables the poor to begin building savings accounts. It is enabling new forms of online philanthropy, where donors can fine-tune their giving to target particular innovations. And it is beginning to spawn new systems through which communities teach one another—as with the Digital Green agriculture project highlighted in Chapter 3. Artificial intelligence can forecast disease outbreaks, develop new methods for diagnosis, and help small farmers prepare for drought. Social media allows people to share ideas and connect as never before about parental concerns, civic engagement, or nonprofit fundraising. The list goes on and on.

Yet, because data technology is literally everywhere, it can be difficult for an activist to step back and determine how best to use it. Often, we are so enamored of new capabilities that we deploy them in less-than-efficient ways. Right now, we have thousands of digital tools that are nowhere near scale, being used through an uncoordinated patchwork of programs. In some countries, we see health workers carrying five different mobile devices in their backpacks to log data for five different diseases. In many countries, none of these tools can communicate with any other, so we have thousands of databases being created with little clarity, coordination, or vision for where the data is leading. Not surprisingly, that has led some to pushback against this "all pilots and no passengers" phenomenon, which could undercut momentum around improvement.

The new generation of practical activists will need to untangle this knot and figure out which digital investments to prioritize. They will need to think more about interoperability, coherency, adaptation, and affordability. This requires a shift from envisioning the tool itself to assessing its fit for the underlying system in which it will be used.

Increased access to data also raises the very real possibility of nefarious misuse of personal information. Our digital revolution—particularly the rise of social media—has revealed dangers that few took seriously at its heady beginnings. Not even my friend, Filipina journalist and activist Maria Ressa, who was celebrated by *Time* magazine for fighting political corruption enabled by political leaders' use of social media, foresaw the threats that technology can produce.

Maria is a book unto herself. A brilliant bundle of energy and ideas packed into a wiry frame barely five feet tall, her coverage of terrorist networks while working as CNN's bureau chief in the Philippines attracted worldwide attention. And in 2012, when she left television to start the online news site Rappler, Maria was a huge fan of technology. As a means of sharing information, she believed it would spur civic engagement and bring people together in "communities of action" to work on world issues like climate change. "I drank the Kool-Aid. I looked at it completely positively," she says. "I believed technology could jumpstart development in the Philippines—until 2016, when tech turned against us."

Maria is referring to what happened when her scrappy, young news crew at Rappler began publishing stories that angered Philippine president Rodrigo Duterte. They pushed further, demonstrating how Facebook had been weaponized by Duterte's administration and others to make disinformation about Rappler and other targets go viral. In short order, Maria was arrested and jailed—multiple times—even as her work continued to be celebrated around the world.

Technology has evolved so rapidly that it is outstripping our ability to build it in a way that corrects for humanity's biases and frailties, Maria worries. Already, several studies are criticizing the inherent racial and gender biases in some AI algorithms. Particularly in the so-called global south, where emerging democracies are still weak, lack of governance over digital and data tools is getting people killed, imprisoned, and harassed. "Colonialism never died, it just moved online," Maria says. She sees these consequences every single day. She now thinks of democracy like a body, and sees social media as a virus that's infected it. Ironically, the first robust efforts to put any check on these life-or-death powers has come in response to the global pandemic COVID-19, she observes.

Maria has not given up hope for the promise of tech. She is, at heart, fascinated with its potential. But her experience about its ability to reshape society in horrifying ways provides a visceral, cautionary tale. "Facebook has broken democracy in many countries around the world, including mine," she says.

Back in the 1990s, at the dawn of the tech age, I didn't necessarily envision any of these risks. But I did sense the scope of possibility unfolding before us. I remember the precise moment this dawned on me. It was during the mid-1990s, at a conference in Sonoma for the CEOs of emerging tech companies, and we were all sitting around one of those fake campfires with our glasses of wine. I was there as the leader of Corbis, which aimed to make digital images of art and photography available to media companies worldwide. Where I'd grown up, there was no museum to go look at a Degas or Picasso, but now this "information superhighway" was going to allow anyone to view any painting they might want to see at any time. Others sitting around that firepit were talking about banking without ever going to banks, shopping without leaving your home. At the time, it was head-spinning.

I wasn't thinking yet about how technology could help poor people or advance a social mission. But I could see how disruptive it would be. Already, Corbis was forcing us to rethink ethics around intellectual property, collecting digital images, and sharing them commercially—just as we do today with personal data. Back then, the mere concept of digitizing art was considered heresy. But I could feel the wave of energy coursing through these discussions. A few of us even got together to create an organization called Npower, so we could put technology in the hands of nonprofits. This digital revolution was going to mean something to social activists—even if we didn't quite know what it would be—and we wanted to help them take part. I had the sense of watching something powerful unfold that was going to change the world. Twenty-five years later, I feel the same thing when thinking about the possibilities for artificial intelligence and quantum computing.

Though we've moved past questions about people's rights to view the Great Masters on their laptops, data technology is still often debated as an emblem of unqualified Good or dystopian Evil. Neither category is accurate, in my view, because neither is appropriately nuanced. Make no mistake, I am convinced that AI and advanced digital tools will become part of the fabric of social change work, and that their potential good outweighs the risks. But there are very challenging digital minefields that all social activists will need to navigate as we move forward. With better tools to gather, analyze, and predict health outcomes, our methods for managing that information become that much more important.

Consider control of personal data. Certainly, individuals should "own" their information to some degree, but not exclusively. What about data that could be disaggregated and used at the population level to manage a disease outbreak? Or tools that could track people's movements to enforce social distancing? All national health systems with integrated data sets will need to consider government versus personal rights. Private-sector access to consumer information raises similar worries. We've pretty much accepted that Amazon will track our shopping preferences and use them to target us for new products we might want to buy. But what happens when data collected for one purpose is used for another? What if a government that collects health data on HIV/AIDs simultaneously declares that it plans to round up and imprison gay men?

Of paramount concern to me currently is the manipulation of social media to create false narratives—about the dangers of vaccination, for example. Spreading incorrect information about inoculation has already resulted in children dying of easily preventable diseases. Misuse of personal data on social media will be one of the major challenges of the next decade. Already, we have seen the results of foreign interference in our elections and, as Maria Ressa's experience shows, of social media being used as a divisive political tool.

From the perspective of equity, there are still millions of people around the world who lack access to technological tools as well as the electricity, connectivity, and training to make them useful. Sometimes a community's health problems, like stunting and its effect on brain development, are so severe that many citizens can't even use technology. Even in emerging lower-middle-class countries, many community organizations are unequipped to keep up with the rapid pace of technological transformation. If we neglect to bring everyone on board the digital wave, there is serious danger that those at the diamond's bottom tip will fall too far behind to catch up.

Because the world's technological transformation has been evolving for decades, it's hard to remember how much resistance we encountered at the outset. But it's instructive to keep in mind as we push forward. We don't think twice about using a credit card to buy something online today, but I recall trudging through endless discussions about how to build consumer confidence in online commerce. We laugh at this now, but the social sector is still very much behind the curve on visionary thinking about ways to use technology to advance human development.

For instance, though many families in the poorest communities of Africa and Asia have mobile phones, they are only at the nascent stage of using these tools to promote their own well-being. Some of that is the result of weak infrastructure and the inconsistent availability of power, internet, and affordable tools. But it is also due to fragmented resources and conflicting priorities. Many places are still "data deserts" with little reliable information on their populations, land ownership, health or education outcomes. Applying artificial intelligence in settings where data is collected without consistency, rigor, or adequate oversight—such as frontline clinics with poor systems and overworked volunteers—could result in perverse outcomes: bad data in, bad data out.

All this to say, the technological frontier raises serious concerns that need to be front-of-mind as we embrace this new world. But embrace it we must, building bridges between tech evangelists and nonbelievers. Perhaps the most important thing I learned in the early days of the internet was that to make technology relevant and useful, we need to build teams that join across different disciplines, with different viewpoints.

This was standard practice at McKinsey. When consulting on digital innovation in global development, we intentionally designed teams linking technology experts with authorities in health (or agriculture or education), and others who had backgrounds in regulatory affairs, marketing, or behavioral science. We did the same thing at PATH. These teams were not without management challenges, since people brought such different mindsets to the table, but I've always felt that this cross-discipline approach made our products and services more successful.

In contrast, a few years ago while visiting Google's life science innovation team I noticed that there were only software engineers around the table. They had many imaginative ideas for malaria control and elimination, but not a single expert on the disease itself. They presumed they could figure out those details on their own. "We'll Google malaria if we need to know more," they said. You will not be surprised to learn that they have had little impact on the global fight against malaria.

Given the digital programs I've described in this chapter and the overall growth of tech innovation, some readers may wonder why I point to it as a new undercurrent powering activism—technology, after all, is not a new story. Yet we've barely scratched the surface of its potential impact. Many of these capabilities are still quite novel in remote corners of the globe. More broadly, we are only beginning to develop a sophisticated sense for the way digital networks, mobile devices, and data analytics can interconnect for widespread impact in social programs. Even with thousands of fascinating digital pilots under way, we can point to only a handful of examples where these tools are shaping global development at scale. In truth, the sheer volume of innovation in digital and data is perhaps our most underreported challenge.

No, bits and bytes won't cure cancer or stop HIV. But they may be essential to quickly develop a COVID-19 vaccine or finally realize the promise of universal health coverage envisioned in the United Nations' Sustainable Development Goals for 2030. Data and technology are helping us to understand and visualize problems differently, empowering both consumers and communities in ways that line up with some of the other undercurrents I've discussed—particularly the push toward locally driven solutions and a greater voice for people long denied a seat at the decision-making table.

The opportunity to empower people and transform our society through digital technology is staggering. But it will require the next generation of practical activists to think very differently about their work. They will need to be savvy negotiators, balancing the potential for doing good against the possibilities for abuse of that power. In some cases, this will necessitate changing laws, policies, and protocols. On the ground, it will mean that every program be examined through the lens of digital soundness: Are you using the best available tools? Will they operate in concert with others, integrating information from multiple sources to make truly meaningful observations? What about your methods for capturing the data—are you disaggregating it for gender, race, age, or other factors? Are you managing and sharing it with appropriate caution? Can we improve an existing project by applying digital technology?

I encourage all activists to embrace the potential, rather than fear its consequences. Because here we are; there is no going back. The technology revolution will demand much faster decision making from our sector, given the speed of innovation and lack of regulatory oversight. It will require engagement with the private companies driving much of that innovation. And ultimately, it will mean ceding more power to individuals—consumers, patients, students, farmers—to make decisions about their own health, education, and finances. People may debate the role of technology in social innovation. But it underlies everything we do.

As Klaus Schwab, founder of the World Economic Forum, writes in *The Fourth Industrial Revolution*, "Technology is not an exogenous force over which we have no control. We are not constrained by a binary choice between 'accept and live with it' and 'reject and live without it.' Instead, take dramatic technological change as an invitation to reflect about who we are and how we see the world. The more we think about how to harness the technology revolution, the more we will examine ourselves and the underlying social models that these technologies embody and enable, and the more we will have an opportunity to shape the revolution in a manner that improves the state of the world."

6

The Surprisingly Sexy Middle

Crossing the Valleys of Death to Scale Innovation

Nearly every problem has been solved by someone, somewhere. The challenge of the twenty-first century is to find out what works, and scale it up.

—President Bill Clinton

EVERY DAY, INVENTORS are conceiving extraordinary solutions to address the problems of our world. They are creating new drugs and vaccines for patients in need; digital devices that allow students in remote settings access to the same information as those in major urban centers; tools that help farmers reap larger crops; and innovative financial services that offer the poor a ladder out of poverty. Every week, I see fresh evidence of this dazzling pipeline of innovation through the scores of email pitches that come my way from activists, students, and entrepreneurs seeking support for their frequently brilliant ideas. Every year, we champion extraordinary new inventions identified through contests sponsored by groups like the Skoll Foundation, the Bill & Melinda Gates Foundation, government innovation authorities, and the TED Conference. The energy and funding generated by this attention has been a tremendous shot in the arm.

Yet when I take a step back, my excitement sometimes wanes. There are already hundreds of incredible, effective solutions sitting on laboratory shelves or floundering in pilot programs—ingenious ideas for saving or improving the lives of millions, maybe billions, of people that never get beyond the proof-of-concept phase. In global health alone, there are thousands of medical products—tested, safe, and ready to shield people from disease—that are not reaching those who need them the most. In education, innumerable approaches to helping children learn at an individualized pace get stuck in eternal trial stages, failing to achieve widespread adoption. Whatever the sector—agriculture, climate, finance, health, job training, or schooling—too many social innovations, even when proven successful, fail to scale. Instead, they languish, unused or incomplete.

Why? Because they are stymied by what social entrepreneurs refer to as the infamous twin valleys of death, a gauntlet of complicated tasks that all innovators must navigate to take ideas to scale. The first of these valleys involves getting a product or service from the drawing board to launch pad; the second, and often more harrowing, is moving from launch to widespread uptake. No matter how promising, innovations repeatedly fail to achieve significant social impact because of the treacherous demands for testing, adapting, funding, validating, regulating, licensing, launching, and marketing that comprise the valleys of death. Together, these hurdles effectively kill one great idea after another because we haven't focused enough attention on navigating those landmines to successfully bring exciting innovations to scale.

This undercurrent in social activism—scaling solutions—is the most persistently underrecognized and underfunded, to the peril of us all. In the decade ahead, practical activists will need to change that and spend a lot more time, money, and energy bringing proven solutions to broad use.

There are many reasons for this lag in knowledge around scaling. For one thing, it is messy and unglamorous. Scholars often describe it as the journey between two critical points on the "value chain" of getting great ideas to communities. At one end of the chain is the invention (or "ideation," as some label it): developing a new gadget, enterprise, or cure. Everyone loves this part. It's creative and exciting. It generates words like "breakthrough," "genius," and "founder." Though this first-mile portion of the trek is usually fraught with enormous difficulties, it's also the part that creates celebrities who win Nobel Prizes and MacArthur Genius awards. The last-mile delivery at the other end of the chain—bringing products and services to people who need them—is also immensely gratifying for anyone who wants to see change happen "on the ground." These two points, the moment of discovery inside an inventor's garage and the sounds, many years later, of clean water arriving in a rural household for the first time, are the stuff of movies, books, and splashy news stories. They are full of true heroics. The distance between them is the part we never see, the slog through the middle. It is usually erratic and looks more like a zigzagging pinball than a smoothly bowled strike. It often lasts for decades. Almost always, it involves complex partnerships, frustrating setbacks, and financial worry. Along this journey from blueprint to impact, innumerable crevasses and potholes swallow brilliant ideas whole.

For far too long, we social innovators have been beguiled by the romance at either end of the value chain. But essential work and enormous need lie in the treacherous middle: that trek through endless rounds of testing, refinement, and approvals. Then the launch, distribution, adoption, and training of users at the other end. All this needs to happen before your brilliant concept can affect millions of lives and change the world.

Consider, for example, the three-decade journey of the Vaccine Vial Monitor (VVM), a simple technology designed to ensure that vaccines are effective by the time they reach children in the developing world. The first thing to know is that vaccines must be kept cold to be effective. But it's a long trip from a vaccine manufacturer's highly regulated loading dock to the child in a rural clinic, and avoiding heat along the way isn't always possible. For many years, this reality created a whole new tragedy: despite valiant efforts to formulate these life-saving interventions, make them affordable, and transport them across the world; despite the cooperation of government agencies, community organizations, pharmaceutical companies, and funders, thousands of kids who received immunization were likely dying because somewhere along the way a vial of vaccine had been exposed to too much heat, rendering it useless. Worse, it was impossible for health workers to reliably discern whether that had happened. So how to ensure potency inside each vial?

Lore has it that a lab worker from PATH, heading home after work one day in the late 1970s, stopped off at a grocery store to buy chicken for dinner and noticed the perishable food sticker on his poultry, indicating whether it had been thawed or not. He wondered if the same technology could be applied to vaccines. What if there were some sort of easy-to-read temperature sensor affixed to each vial that could tell any health worker whether the chemicals inside were still viable? With this idea, work began on what is now known as the Vaccine Vial Monitor, a thermochromic label with a small square that changes color when exposed to heat. Think of an at-home pregnancy test, or one of those pop-up readers that alerts you when your Thanksgiving turkey is ready. At a glance, any health worker can see whether the vaccine inside has been kept sufficiently cool.

Back in the lab at PATH, everyone could see that this was a brilliant solution, ingenious in its simplicity and, really, just a clever adaptation of food-safety technologies already in use. The benefits would be twofold: aside from children receiving only viable vaccines, health workers would no longer waste perfectly good vials by throwing out those they were uncertain about. It took 10 years and an unusual partnership with a food-safety startup to develop a temperature sensor that was both accurate for a variety of vaccines and acceptable to the World Health Organization (WHO), which must approve any health innovation used in public markets. An entire decade, just to cross the first valley of death.

One of the initial challenges was locking down a manufacturer that could make this tool at the requisite volume while keeping costs low. Businesses depend on reliable demand and financial projections—the value proposition—but it was impossible to present an accurate cost–benefit forecast because PATH, which was guiding the whole process, had no tools to definitively measure how many children were receiving heat-corrupted vaccines or dying for lack of protection. This made it difficult to quantify the benefits, either in saving wasted vaccine or safeguarding human health. Also, different vaccines have different temperature tolerances so creating a single indicator that would work for all required still more years of work. Meanwhile, much of the world had adequate refrigeration so demand for the innovation was spotty. Are you beginning to grasp the hurdles involved in trying to do good at scale?

Tackling high-stakes problems that seem insurmountable is what practical activists do, however. In most cases, you'll never know their names. But one of them is Debra Kristensen, a former product manager at a medical devices firm who had never worked in global health before joining PATH. Kristensen's primary tool was an ironclad belief that simple changes to the ways we handle vaccine distribution would make an enormous difference to humanity.

A major breakthrough in the journey of the VVM came when PATH and a small New Jersey startup focused on food safety began working together on the project. I have alluded throughout this book to the critical importance of partnerships, and that is not some sort of feel-good palaver. Partnerships are about brass-tacks practicality. There is no advancement without them. This story is a great example. Ted Prusik, co-founder of the New Jersey company then called LifeLines Technologies, later Temptime, was open to the idea of piloting a temperature monitor for vaccines because he saw the possibilities for expansion. Prusik was already supplying temperature indicators to a supermarket chain in France; diversifying into healthcare presented a potentially lucrative new opportunity. With a $25,000 purchase order from PATH, he agreed to make 10,000 temperature monitors for polio vaccine.

Now PATH had the concept approved and a business partner aboard. But we'd spent more than a decade on this project, and there was still a long way to go. After a year of work, Temptime's scientists were still struggling, and the company's board of directors was beginning to ask some hard questions. Prusik told our team that he was ready to pull the plug.

This is where relationships come in. PATH's leadership flew from Seattle to New Jersey to meet with Temptime. They offered no new business arrangement, just described the enormous market and possibilities for impact on the lives of millions of children. Even 25 years later, Prusik gets emotional thinking about it. "I still remember the meeting in the room when we said we were giving up," he told me not long ago. "I still get choked up." Pushing his misgivings aside, Prusik agreed to work a few months more, and during that time Temptime scientists cracked the code. I shudder to think what might have happened if PATH had been unable to make the meaning of this endeavor clear to Prusik, or if he hadn't been passionate enough about it to hold off Temptime's board. Sometimes success turns on a razor's edge.

Meanwhile, PATH and the WHO were trying to encourage other companies to develop VVMs, partly to increase competition and keep prices low and partly to create a backstop in case Temptime ever had production problems. Kristensen, now PATH's Director of Vaccine Technology Strategy and Policy, was talking with 3M, Bowater, Rexam, Albert Browne, CCL Label, and Sensitech. All were interested. A few even developed prototypes.

But in the end, none signed on. Between the technical demands, low-pricing requirements, and lack of a clear value proposition, the drawbacks were just too daunting.

Temptime had found reason to press forward. But translating the company's heat sensor label from a clever idea into billions of units required resources well beyond those of a tech startup. Government and donors to the rescue: over the next five years, USAID steadily supported the testing and impact studies necessary to move this project forward. Without that backbone of public funding, there is no way VVMs would have become a reality.

There were still more obstacles to clear. Now we had a product and someone to make it, but the main buyer of public sector vaccines is UNICEF, and officers there had harbored reservations about the project from the start. They did not feel comfortable about Temptime as the sole supplier—what if there was a disruption or delay at the company's plant? What if Temptime decided to raise its prices? And initially, UNICEF did not mandate VVMs for use on all vaccines. Kristensen, celebrating prematurely after UNICEF lent its initial approval in 1990, repeatedly found herself back at the negotiating table fielding questions from the two dozen pharmaceutical manufacturers that would be putting VVMs on their labels—each incurring extra costs, and new worries about liability, without any increase in profit. "It was a tough time," she says, looking back. "You might think that putting a label on something is not a big deal, but it is. It reminds me of that song 'Fifty Ways to Leave Your Lover'; it seemed like there were 50 ways to leave VVMs."

Sometimes, these things come down to the personalities around a table. Kristensen credits a team of former architects working at the WHO to improve the international cold-chain with making the difference. "They believed in the need for this technology," she says. "They were not going to give up."

The valleys of death are vast. They're treacherous, and often tedious. Even after PATH went to extraordinary lengths to help Temptime stay afloat, there was still the matter of training health workers to correctly read the new VVMs. If you don't have the trust of people on the ground, all your work is for naught.

By 2017, PATH finally had outcomes that could quantify the value of this innovation. We were able to show that during two decades of use, preserving vaccines had likely protected hundreds of thousands of lives. Today these dime-sized monitors have been used on more than eight billion vials. As Bill Gates said about the project, "Sometimes it's the simple ideas that make all the difference." But consider: work on VVMs started in 1979, entered the market 17 years later, and did not enjoy widespread use for another decade. That's almost 30 years from initial concept to realizing a benefit at scale.

The VVM journey is not a story of brilliant scientific breakthroughs. No Nobel Prize will be bestowed for adapting food-safety technology to everyday healthcare. Nowadays, most health experts just take this advance for granted. VVM, really, is a story about the complexity of the middle and the fortitude, creativity, and patience needed to get even simple ideas across the valley of death. It's a story about the many people from all corners of the world—health regulators at the WHO and UNICEF, businessmen at Temptime, policy experts and product engineers at nongovernmental organizations like PATH—who had to align around the basic goal of ensuring vaccine potency. These partners, in turn, had to convince 28 pharmaceutical companies to buy and use the VVMs.

It's rarely elegant, this behind-the-scenes work of building partnerships, raising funds, convincing regulators, adapting tools, testing markets, and aligning agendas. Not surprisingly, lots of activists prefer to concentrate on first- or last-mile heroics. They think that's the cool part, inventing things or watching innovation actually change lives. But from my perspective, the middle is really the sexy part. It's all about working collaboratively, solving problems, and getting stuff done. It is where I have spent the bulk of my career. And it is absolutely critical to scaling any innovation.

Aside from fortitude and diplomacy, scaling takes money—often millions of dollars to get a solution fully tested, approved, and distributed. (VVMs, for instance, took more than $2 million in public funds; a new vaccine might take several hundred million.) Few donors, however, can afford that level of investment or the risks that go with it. Typically, they have been more interested in attaching themselves to big ideas or measurable outcomes, rather than supporting the messy processes to get there. Scaling has neither the sheen of a shiny new app nor the political potency of advancing discussions around equity. And the deliverables are difficult to quantify. But developing deeper know-how around this part of social innovation is crucial for practical activists, and I think it will become a major undercurrent powering global development through the next decade.

Why is this idea important now? Scaling innovation is hardly a new concept, after all; the social sector has been doing it with great impact for a long time. One reason for new attention today is investment cycles. During the past 20 years, philanthropy, government, and nonprofits have funneled hundreds of billions of dollars into global health and development. Many new players—like the Gates Foundation, Bloomberg Philanthropies, Wellcome Trust, Dangote Foundation, Tata Trust, Hilton Foundation, Global Fund, Gavi, and PEPFAR—are stepping onto the field. This new funding, coupled with significant contributions from billionaire entrepreneurs and emerging economies, has created a virtuous cycle of increased political commitment to the aspirations outlined in the UN Sustainable Development Goals (SDGs). It has generated thousands of new products and services to improve human well-being. In fact, support of social entrepreneurship around human-centered design has never been better.

But to make these extraordinary investments pay off, we now need to push more of the resulting innovations across the valleys of death. That means moving beyond the curse of "pilotitis." A derisive term often used by activists, pilotitis describes the plethora of one-off projects that may benefit a small region or discrete population but never get funded to achieve sustainable, broad-based impact. The phenomenon has become so frustrating to some countries that they are declaring moratoriums on anything other than end-to-end solutions that can be seamlessly integrated into existing systems. But without adoption at the systems level, generally by a government, many of these promising innovations eventually wither. This is why more attention to the sexy middle of the innovation journey is so urgent. Now is the time to focus on selecting, funding, and ensuring that the best ideas are nurtured to generate the large-scale effects for which they were intended.

That focus is boosted by new collaborative funding models like TED's Audacious Project, Co-Impact, Blue Meridian Partners, or the MacArthur Foundation's 100&Change program, all designed to solve problems at scale. These efforts create big-donor investment platforms aimed at supporting full, soup-to-nuts solutions for improving global education, energy production, agriculture, climate action, and health. A great example is the $100 million that was granted in 2018 to the early-learning project Ahlan Simsim. Funded by MacArthur and the LEGO Foundation, this program joins the Sesame Workshop, familiar to anyone who's watched children's television, with the International Rescue Committee. The aim: to mitigate trauma and develop social-emotional skills among 9.4 million kids across the Middle East affected by the Syrian conflict. Ahlan Simsim ("welcome Sesame" in Arabic) was MacArthur's first 100&Change contest winner, which Sesame Workshop claims to be the largest early-learning initiative in the history of humanitarian response. It involves a lot more than television. From inception, the project was designed as one that would be intense enough to change lives while maintaining the kind of cost efficiencies that allow for scaling. Alongside home visits and school lessons, a key component of Ahlan Simsim is measuring outcomes so that the entire world can learn more about the best interventions for kids in crisis settings—wherever they may be.

Urgency around getting solutions to scale is now palpable. Across the social sector, people have begun to refer to the 2020s as the "decade of delivery." That is, in part, a result of the ticking clock we all sense around the need to do something—fast—about climate change and growing economic inequity. There is also the looming 2030 deadline to deliver on at least some of the bold commitments in the UN's SDGs, such as eradicating extreme poverty worldwide, protecting our oceans, and ensuring universal access to sexual and reproductive healthcare. Some of this push for speedier results comes from the power of our new digital tools to accelerate the work. All of it speaks to the critical importance of more know-how in bringing solutions to scale.

COVID-19 dramatically underscored the need for more know-how around this undercurrent. The sheer volume of tragedy unfolding at warp speed made it a real-time case study on the challenges of scaling, particularly scaling quickly. In the space of a few fraught weeks, the world's attention was suddenly riveted on the question of how to select, test, and adapt interventions. But, as someone who was working frantically behind the scenes to deploy my skills in practical activism like never before, I can tell you that scrambling to collect surgical gowns and masks from suppliers across the globe while navigating the competitive, complicated world of procurement did not, in the moment, feel terribly sexy.

During the first few months, as cases and deaths escalated dramatically, media reports pointed out appalling shortfalls in testing equipment, personal protective gear, and other supplies. But they generally revealed a lack of appreciation for the difficulty of steering through the rules of supply-chain management, procurement, international cargo transportation, and the endless list of other requirements for getting them delivered to health workers. Understandably impatient, many first-mile inventors came up with clever adaptations for new types of tests, masks, ventilators, and medical oxygen. But they were often surprised at the regulatory, distribution, and coordination hurdles that followed.

In a few cases, we were able to expedite ideas. Because swabs used to test for COVID-19 were initially in short supply, scientists came up with a stopgap by combining Q-tip–like materials with a modified saline solution to achieve the same effect. Others developed 3-D printer models for mask-making that were blessed by government authorities. Applications to enable engagement between citizens and health authorities scaled quickly, helping with communication about the virus and the information needed to help manage its spread. But a veritable deluge of ingenious digital tools, apps, and algorithms aimed to solve some aspect of the pandemic sat waiting. Government leaders, entrepreneurs, and corporate executives who'd never shown much interest in these complexities before were now intently focused on this problem; they couldn't understand why it took so long to get new tests approved, or new products launched, or new tools adapted in the context of a global crisis. In the midst of the tragedy, I could not help believing that COVID-19 would ultimately spur better systems to handle these middle-of-the-value-chain obstacles, focusing policymakers and activists on ways to accelerate the scaling of life-saving interventions for the future.

In the moment, of course, talk is cheap. Everyone scrambling to confront COVID-19 could see that it would take real work to devise better ways of moving innovation through the Byzantine journey toward impact at scale. Whether that involves developing a new vaccine, testing diagnostics or drugs, retooling health systems for massive screening, or reorganizing hospitals and health workforces to address future epidemics, the grueling realities of this work have come home to the public as never before.

Emphasizing the delivery of innovation is not to say that research and development should stop—not at all. We still have huge riddles to solve, and we will need serious scientific investment to get there. We need to find cures for cancer, effective vaccines for

HIV and universal flu, noncarbon energy sources, and new methods for water desalination. Don't even get me started on addressing homelessness and addiction; we are in dire want of new ideas to tackle those social challenges. We need to invent better models for helping children with learning disabilities and design financial products that will create more agency for women. Yes, emphatically, to all of this.

But we must also rethink our tendency to overinvest in shiny objects, disproportionally committing funds to R&D when what we really need is more emphasis on adapting existing solutions to provide greater access to more people. The VVM, which used food safety science to tackle a health problem, is a classic example of what I mean. Another comes from inventors at PATH who modified the basic functions of CPAP machines, often used to help with sleep apnea, for helping newborns with breathing problems. Respiratory infections, a leading cause of infant mortality in the world's poorest communities, claim millions of babies each year. But developers figured out that rigging a miniature CPAP with a small plastic device designed using a 3-D printer to blend air and pure oxygen could save these children's lives, or prevent neurological impairment, at very low cost.

What allows some ideas to scale while others fail? Part of the answer is money. A 2018 paper from the Tides Foundation notes that while most philanthropic grants range between US$50,000 and $500,000, it takes a lot more than that to build the infrastructure, hire teams, develop models, and sustain the collaborations required to bring an idea from the laboratory to fruition on the ground. Also, models for building multi-sectoral partnerships, navigating legislative or regulatory processes, or undertaking the extensive research necessary to demonstrate effectiveness lack the linkage to direct impact that comes from funding service delivery. And sometimes the solutions simply remain too expensive for the targeted community or buyers.

But money is by no means the whole story. Many well-intentioned ideas stall due to inventors' failure to listen to the communities or users on the ground; a lack of government approvals; a poor fit between a product and its target market; a lack of infrastructure to build out the innovation; a dearth of data on the value of the innovation; and partnership management problems. We study these challenges in my class at Stanford, exploring ways to anticipate, avoid, or mitigate the hurdles. Of course, some ideas are just plain bad.

Consider the PlayPump, a playground-sized toy built for children and attached to a water pump. It looked something like a whirlybird. The idea was that kids would leap onto this contraption, spin round, and simultaneously pump water for an entire village—or so went the pitch. The World Bank loved it. A US$60 million global campaign launched in 2006 promised that harnessing children's energy at play could bring clean drinking water to 10 million people in sub-Saharan Africa within four years.

But no one seemed to have spent much time considering the value proposition to the targeted communities. The $14,000 cost per PlayPump would have paid for three conventional hand pumps that produced similar output. Nor did anyone pause to note that generating enough water for a village meant that its children would need to "play" on the pump for more than 24 hours a day. Four years after its emergence to great fanfare on the world stage, PlayPump International was shuttered.

Around the same time the One Laptop Per Child initiative from the MIT Media Lab promised to transform education by distributing low-cost, low-power laptops to children across the developing world. This is the kind of idea that social entrepreneurs and donors love. It was catchy, high-profile, and frugal. It involved many companies sharing the load, and would evangelize for computer literacy worldwide, which spoke to the economic interests of every firm involved. Yet many of the communities targeted for this program had problems far more pressing than learning to work a trackpad—such as lack of reliable electricity. The anticipated results never materialized.

I started teaching a course on scaling social innovation at Stanford because I kept seeing this gap between the thinking of committed young activists, who'd had fantastic last-mile experiences everywhere from rural Ghana to East Palo Alto, and their keen interest in designing a new innovation and starting a social enterprise. What we needed, I felt, was a way to connect the dots between that idealism and the reality of what it takes to bring innovation to the world at large. I can't tell you how many PowerPoint presentations I've sat through that detail the intricate design and alleged value of a great idea, then conclude with a small asterisk on the right-hand side of the final slide that says "scale up." As if this were as simple as flipping a switch.

I live in that asterisk. It has been the locus of most of my work, and I can tell you that people who dash off the word "scale" rarely consider the critical role of policymakers in spreading innovation. Nor do they always appreciate how to create a market to drive demand for their products—often in places where markets have failed. Some have thought very little about regulatory hurdles or possible partnerships, let alone the idea of handing off their beloved invention to another organization that might be able to expand its impact more effectively. That's likely because all those valley-of-death endeavors are messy, nonlinear, and usually thankless. They lack the seductive elegance of a brilliant idea. But for the practical activist, that asterisk is your battleground. It's where the rubber meets the road. It's where you accomplish the real work that leads to positive change—the sexy middle.

I always begin my class by asking students to read Atul Gawande's wonderful 2013 article from *The New Yorker*, "Slow Ideas." A surgeon, journalist, and thought leader in health, Gawande dissects the forces behind the spread—or stall—of advances in medicine by focusing on the path of two innovations in surgery from the nineteenth century. The first was handwashing.

It's universal to us now. But you'd be amazed at the resistance that met this simple, proven, lifesaving practice. The other was use of anesthesia during surgery, which spread as rapidly as contagion itself.

In 1846, Gawande writes, there was no such thing as anesthesia, and it was standard practice during surgery for attendants to physically restrain patients as they thrashed and screamed. But a Boston dentist discovered that inhaling ether rendered clients calm and quiet in the chair, completely transforming his practice. Within three months of a published report about this, anesthesia had been adopted for use in most major European cities. Within six months, it was commonplace across much of the world—just six months!

Difficult surgeries, however, were hardly a problem when compared with the number of people who died after undergoing procedures—up to half of all patients. In the 1860s, Scottish surgeon Joseph Lister surmised that the cause of these deaths was infection, most likely from germs, and that carbolic acid could destroy them. He took a few years to devise ways of using carbolic acid in handwashing and tool sterilization, saw dramatically lowered rates of infection and death among his patients, and presented these findings in *The Lancet* in 1867.

Silence.

Two decades later, surgeons continued to operate in "black frockcoats stiffened with the blood and viscera" of previous patients. They saw this as evidence of a busy practice, a badge of honor. It was another generation before sterilization and handwashing became routine.

Why would this be? Neither innovation was unduly expensive—indeed, as Gawande points out, having more patients survive surgery meant that more medical bills would be paid. The answer illuminates many of the nuances in scaling innovation, even today.

First, the problem addressed by handwashing—germs—was invisible, rather than the shrieking immediacy solved by anesthesia. Secondly, while both advances improved life for patients, only one made things easier for doctors, who would be employing the new practices.

My takeaway? Think of the enormous problems confronting our world—climate change, worsening income inequality, lack of education. The solutions to each will involve a level of inconvenience or sacrifice, our equivalent of a doctor taking time for handwashing. To scale a good idea, then, we need to think carefully about the people using it and design for what makes sense within their customs and culture. Even something as low-tech and cost-free as "kangaroo care"—placing a newborn baby on a mother's bare chest, which has been proven to help infants regulate body temperature and build immunity—is a struggle to "sell" in many hospitals because it is counter to tradition and the problems it solves are not immediately visible.

Gawande writes about the many ways of prodding people toward embracing innovation—whether by asking them to shift their habits, compelling them to do so through threat of punishment, or nudging them forward with incentives. All are aimed at the holy grail for successfully scaling any new idea: sustainable culture change.

One reason so many people ignore the sometimes seemingly unsexy middle of scaling innovation is that the nature of the enterprise is easily confused. Am I talking about bringing a product to the world stage from a private company that has social benefit? Or am I referring to ideas for system change that come from government and the social sector of foundations, nonprofits, and research institutions? The answer is both. Social innovation comes in many forms, all requiring incentives and partnerships in order to scale.

Let me spell out what I mean by social innovations. I think of them as a box with four corners: they must be new; be able to create significant positive social impact, usually for vulnerable or low-resource communities; be sustainable or long-lasting; and be partnerships involving cross-sector collaboration. Is a new product like the Tesla automobile a social innovation? Sure. While the company is a for-profit entity, its innovation was driven by a commitment to addressing environmental concerns and pushing drivers toward using less fossil fuel. Tesla's success necessitated significant work with policymakers in government, first for approval of electric vehicles, then to get electric stations built. Some thinkers split hairs on the definition of social innovation, insisting that impact on the public be the primary rather than secondary motivation. In my class, students always debate this question with strong arguments on either side. I have always pushed for an inclusive interpretation. But either way, the themes and lessons of social innovation can be broadly applied.

With this example in mind, I ask my students to go home, look around, and note some of the items or procedures in their lives that they'd call social innovations—that is, new products or ways of doing things that bolster the common good. Inevitably, they come back talking about civic-minded community groups promoting new initiatives on social media or cool new apps for monitoring health data and exercise on their wristwatches. But one young man mentioned seatbelts. Immediately, everyone got it. The seatbelt is a classic example of social innovation at scale. It took nearly a hundred years between the invention by nineteenth-century English engineer George Cayley and the moment government regulators made seatbelts mandatory in every U.S. car. It was a bit longer, still, before laws like "Click it or ticket" required everyone to use a seatbelt. But now it's simply part of our culture.

I love this example because it underscores the need for an innovation to have buy-in from multiple sectors before it can scale—that is, private enterprise (car companies and seat belt manufacturers); social (through academic research and nonprofits' public safety campaigns) and, finally, government (with policies, standards, and enforcement mechanisms). Think about other social innovations—new education platforms, farming methods, microfinance in the developing world, vaccines and drugs—their journey to scale almost always span this same panoply of actors.

In my class, we spend lots of time talking about the role of these different sectors in scaling social innovation, particularly the powerful part played by government, whether as a regulator, policymaker, funder, purchaser, or champion. Every year, this is the moment when the lightbulb comes on in my students' eyes. Many of them arrive with a strong predisposition against the public sector, believing that innovators should try to avoid it as much as possible given government's reputation for bureaucracy, regulation, and glacial progress. Every year, their biggest aha moment is the realization of how simplistic these biases are and how necessary the public sector is to virtually any successful scaling effort. None of our brilliance matters if we can't deliver it en masse. And that almost always involves government.

Not all social innovations involve inventing a product; innovations in processes, services, and financing matter a lot. Look at the transformation under way in juvenile justice across the United States. Twenty years ago, driven by widespread fears of so-called "super-predator" teenagers, the United States was incarcerating kids at rates of 355 per every 100,000 people. That's about 28,000 young people locked in detention facilities where whatever problems had landed them in legal trouble to begin with only worsened. Many activists noted the grossly disproportionate ways that school discipline was—and still is—leveled on black youth and how this led to more kids of color winding up locked up. The phrase "school-to-prison pipeline" was not just an incendiary rallying cry; it was backed by hard numbers. And it was saddling a generation of young people with criminal records before they were old enough to vote.

The Annie E. Casey Foundation decided to tackle this immense challenge, with the audacious goal of changing the way local communities handled youth crime in all 50 states. That was an enormously tall order since the Casey Foundation is not a government body. It involved marshaling data to prove the point that the overuse of juvenile detention was expensive and counterproductive. It meant educating the public about those findings and inspiring policy changes at the legislative level. To do those things, Casey also needed to present alternatives that would satisfy concerns about public safety.

No doubt, there were many conversations at the foundation about the wisdom of hewing to this campaign over two decades. But it has worked. Today, Casey's system for reducing youth incarceration—which includes screening tools for assessing criminal risk, streamlining case processing, and measuring youth outcomes—has been adopted by nearly every state. Across the country, juvenile detention is down 61 percent from 1999, with no decrease in public safety. "The road to scale inevitably will run through public systems," says Patrick McCarthy, Casey's president during the latter part of this effort. "Decades of experience tell us that a bad system will trump a good program—every time, all the time."

That's why I urge increased focus on our systems for delivering innovation. Within the social sector, one of our biggest impediments to broad-based success has been the reluctance to turn our ideas over to the private sector or government. Clearly, that was a cornerstone of the Casey approach to transforming juvenile justice. But it is all too rare.

This self-limiting mindset is very different from that in private enterprise, where entrepreneurs routinely advance ideas with the expectation that, if successful, they will eventually be handed off to a company with bigger reach. It is extremely rare that a new product or service is created and scaled by the same company. Because founders and inventors are well compensated in these handoffs, most often in the form of a merger or acquisition, the idea of an exit is built into their business model.

Not so much in the social sector, where most of our innovations are targeted to the bottom of our squat diamond, often into places where markets are failing, and therefore have little value in sheer financial terms. There's no traditional valuation model for measuring the worth of a social innovation, and rarely any capital rewarding the social innovator, let alone paying for the cost of these transactions. This inhibits the desire of many social enterprises to let go and allow others to carry their ideas across the second valley of death. It's jaw-dropping, frankly, to consider the enormous sums of money and years of effort devoted to discovering new products that could make a difference in human development, without spending equal effort paving the way for these proven innovations to see the light of day.

Innovation, of course, is not always anchored by a new product or process. Often, large-scale social change is about shifting ideas, and that demands advocacy around public policy. The importance of this work—through mounting information campaigns, educating policymakers, supporting ballot initiatives, and reshaping policies or laws—cannot be overstated. I learned that lesson repeatedly as a gay activist. Despite decades of work on innovative service programs, or funding important causes, or supporting people who had been victimized by discrimination, at the end of the day it was the laws and elections that mattered most. Yet there is a delicacy to these battles—in particular, choosing which to fight—that I sometimes lost sight of in my relentless focus on practical activism.

During the late 1980s and early 1990s, when AIDS was a word that inspired terror, and the idea of same-sex marriage a laughable dream, I joined the national board of Lambda Legal. We were a group of lawyers, mainly, who gathered in New York City to hammer out plans for impact litigation across the country that would advance the cause for equality. At the time, the LBGTQI community faced lawful discrimination on almost every front: housing, employment, insurance, inheritance, military service, healthcare, and marriage. As a movement, we'd been focused mainly on raising money and awareness. But now, it was clear. We needed to map a battleground of legal issues and, consequently, figure out which lawsuit to pursue. What case would truly change our place in America? Should it be something targeting job discrimination, or health access? Military service or anti-sodomy laws? Marriage? We argued bitterly.

My practical side kicked in hard during these nuanced debates. Many of my colleagues felt that fighting the ban on gays and lesbians in the military would win us few points politically, and some were opposed to doing anything to support the national defense establishment. But I was adamant about going after the military service ban, primarily because the Department of Defense was one of the largest employers in the country. Thousands of jobs were potentially at stake. Marriage, on the other hand, seemed like a nonstarter. I just didn't see why recognition for legal unions beyond domestic partnership was important (aside from the financial benefits, like taxes and inheritance, that could be litigated on their own). I honestly thought fighting for marriage rights was, well, romanticizing the movement. In meeting after meeting, I argued that we should focus solely on decriminalizing sodomy and fighting housing and job discrimination. It seemed like the most pragmatic plan of attack. But this was a battle I lost.

In hindsight, it's clear that I missed the importance of marriage as an institution. I didn't understand how politically powerful it would be as a storyline and tool for helping Americans see their LGBTQI neighbors, and the broader community, as fundamentally the same as themselves. And I am thrilled that through political action, court cases, ballot initiatives, and an important U.S. Supreme Court decision, we won this right. It has done more than anything else to shift our status as citizens.

Nevertheless, it is currently still legal to fire or evict LGBTQI people because of their sexual identity in 29 states. It happens all the time. And the impacts of stigma, family rejection, and discriminatory practices are pervasive. In the United States, gay teenagers are four times more likely than straights to attempt suicide. Beyond U.S. borders, the situation is far more dire. In 70 countries, gay relationships are illegal and consenting adults are routinely imprisoned, harassed, and sometimes thrown off roofs (this happened in Syria). In 13 countries, gay people can be legally put to death. Despite all our progress, we have a long way to go.

In working for social change with legislators and other policymakers, the art of compromise is a valuable asset for any practical activist. For example, when I visited the Washington, DC, office of Rep. Ted Yoho to discuss possibilities for bringing more private enterprise into global development work, I knew we were from opposite sides of the political spectrum. I also knew we had very different ideas about foreign aid. Representative Yoho, a Republican from Florida, was an influential member of the libertarian Freedom Caucus, and had come to Congress with a deeply negative view of foreign assistance. Spending government money on economies in the developing world did nothing more than enrich "corrupt foreign bureaucrats" at the expense of U.S. taxpayers, he'd said more than once. That position had helped get him elected and kept him in Washington for four terms.

But I'd asked for a meeting to discuss ways that the private sector—that is, business—could become more involved in development. Rep. Yoho, a small-business owner himself, had already begun to investigate these possibilities. I wanted to help him along.

I also knew that he was a veterinarian, and my childhood in a Montana ranching community gave us some common ground to start from. The work I did wasn't all that different from what goes on at a ranch, I said. Although I was focused on solving big problems around the globe, it all started with realities on the ground. I described PATH's innovation strategies—developing products for the world's poorest communities and scaling them up. I said it involved lots of unglamorous work navigating complicated relationships, facing setbacks, and finding commonality. Sort of like living in a small town. (Or, for that matter, working in politics.)

I was really laying it on. But everything I said was true, and it resonated with Representative Yoho.

He explained his initial concerns about foreign aid and how he'd come to Congress to try and eliminate it. But he'd adjusted those views, now understanding aid as a useful tool for advancing diplomacy and U.S. foreign policy aims.

Exactly, I said. That was why we needed more involvement from the private sector. Business could never take over all global development work because it is so often targeted to places where market forces have failed. But I told Representative Yoho that as more countries advanced from poverty toward the middle class, business—and its rigorous, results-oriented approach—would have an increasingly valuable role.

As we spoke, I stared at the Deep South memorabilia behind the representative's desk—including a stuffed alligator. I was well out of my comfort zone. But Representative Yoho is a smart politician and also, as a veterinarian, a man of science. He responds to numbers, facts, evidence. And those things I had. I told him about PATH's work with U.S. software companies and how it was helping to eliminate malaria through better models for tracking the disease, which lowered unnecessary costs while saving lives. I shared data on ways that government incentives could enable industry to do even more to advance new medicines. We talked through the financial challenges for pharmaceutical companies creating products that had no customer base in the rich world. And I asked if there were ways PATH could help him structure aid legislation to include more commercial interests. In other words, rather than begging for money I approached him as a businessman, discussing strategies, tradeoffs, and opportunity costs.

Representative Yoho was all in. He knew we had very different reasons for wanting more private sector involvement, but he could see where our interests met. And he understood the power in joining forces around a common goal. That's pragmatism in service to activism. And it's the kind of work that is key to scaling solutions.

As our global pyramid continues morphing into a squat diamond and we conceive more ways for involving the private sector in public good, it strikes me that the sexy middle is a wide-open field for a new breed of practical activists—people with know-how in the delicate work of gaining regulatory approvals, or ensuring that supply chains are sustainable, or beefing up more sophisticated methods for creating demand on the ground in the communities we want to help. That means hiring people of more diverse experience and career paths. To get stuff done, we need experts who can speak the language of the UN's SDGs and corporate P&Ls (profit and loss statements) in the same sentence, because it may be health economists or MBAs, not just public health specialists, who can best lead our medical advances through the valleys of death. At McKinsey, we called such activists "tri-sector athletes"—people who had worked in government, business, and social sector enterprises. Their key competency—managing and supporting multisector partnerships—may be the single most critical skill for people committed to broad social change during the next decade.

Practical activists who want to catch this wave will need to focus on:

- Adaptation, not only invention or discovery.
- Demand creation, so that communities are pulling innovation to scale, not only relying what gets pushed down from above.
- Implementation science to test and define what drives demand, and what scales.
- The "second valley of death," that point after approval and before implementation, when a new drug, tool, or process needs a model for widespread uptake. We need to invest a lot more in this part of the chain from formally approving and launching a useful product to having it widely used on the ground.

I close this chapter with the story of my friend Keller Rinaudo, co-founder and CEO of Zipline, a social enterprise that uses drones to deliver medical supplies to difficult-to-reach locations. Keller is something of a wunderkind. Trained in engineering and robotics, he has synthesized software and aviation technologies to build six-foot-tall unmanned aircraft that can fly up to 100 miles, safely drop blood supplies, vaccines, and other medical tools into precise locations, then return to a main distribution center for reuse. Keller is already serving an entire country, Rwanda, with this invention and has expanded into Ghana, with plans for India and, eventually, the United States.

Funded by a bunch of Silicon Valley venture capitalists, Zipline is very much a for-profit company. But it was designed from the beginning with social impact in mind. Initially, Keller traveled to different countries, asking to meet with their ministers of health to learn how, or if, robotics might help their health systems work better. The idea for using drones came out of a conversation Keller had with a researcher in Tanzania, who shared his frustration at the failure of his own attempt at innovation: a method for texting emergency orders for medical supplies into a database. The problem was, Tanzania had no capability to transport those supplies to the remote locations where they were needed, so the concept went nowhere. That's when the lightbulb in Keller's mind turned on. Drones could solve this problem.

Six years later, the concept has been proven. Zipline is working effectively across all of Rwanda, and Keller is continually improving its service, technology, and business model. Now he must scale it—no small matter. Securing an agreement with just one country requires negotiating with the civil aviation authorities who control national airspace; ministers of health who oversee health systems; hospital staff who need to know what to do when robots start dropping medication at their doors; and of course, the communities where all this is taking place. "The easy part was building the technology," Keller says. "Integrating it with a national health system—that's much harder. In some ways, we're building the plane as we fly it."

But Keller is learning fast. It took him more than two years to get Zipline's first site up and running in Rwanda, and another three to establish a second distribution center there. In Ghana, however, Zipline established four of these drone-airport/medical fulfillment centers in just 12 months. Meanwhile, Keller's team is working with the U.S. Department of Defense to use Zipline for delivering medical supplies in war zones and at humanitarian disaster sites. No wonder competitors have begun to buzz around.

Maybe this sounds like another instance of shiny-object innovation fated to expire in the second valley of death. That remains to be seen. But I consider Keller's work an example of adaptation, synthesizing previous technologies to create new answers that could very well disrupt old norms. At scale, he might even displace the need for our beloved VVMs, since drones can deliver vaccines quickly enough that the cold-chain issue disappears.

This is how we move forward, one step building on the next, adapting technology to new ends, disrupting and innovating again.

The Undercurrents Ripple and Converge

Practical Activists Navigating New Waters

Few will have the greatness to bend history itself, but each of us can work to change a small portion of events. It is from numberless diverse acts of courage and belief that human history is shaped. Each time a man stands up for an ideal, or acts to improve the lot of others, or strikes out against injustice, he sends forth a tiny ripple of hope, and crossing each other from a million different centers of energy and daring those ripples build a current which can sweep down the mightiest walls of oppression and resistance.

—Robert F. Kennedy

WHEN I WAS A long-haired teenager working the hayfields, I wrote my first book, *Footsteps in the Mud*, with my cousin Holly. It was a spoof on our lives as high school student-irrigators in small-town Montana, circa 1970. While touched with an embarrassing dose of adolescent martyrdom, a quick re-read today reveals that we did understand some profound things about water: its force, flow, and fickle nature that can make the difference between abundance and scarcity. Most of all, we recognized the way water spreads, how it moves outward from distant mountain snow packs, trickling into steams that become rushing creeks that lead to surging rivers, shaping life wherever it passes en route to the place where all these fingers converge. The job of an irrigator, we wrote, was to use nature's currents in ways that would nourish the fields while conserving as much water as possible. Even as kids we created metaphors about water's rhythm and power as it wended inexorably downstream.

I remembered that book while working on this somewhat more ambitious effort, noticing parallels between the natural phenomenon I described then and the social undercurrents—economic, technological, and cultural—that I see today, all of these forces flowing together to generate change. They will not always flow steadily or in a consistent direction, as we have seen with wavering commitments to equity. But I hope I've demonstrated how energy from one current can drive another, generating propulsion. My wish is that the activist in each of us realizes the array of opportunities for tapping this momentum to turn our outrage into practical action.

With that idea in mind, I'd like to share another PATH story. It shows how all the undercurrents are at work when we successfully create lasting impact that changes lives.

The global challenge in this case: nutritional deficiencies among poor populations. That reality affects two billion people worldwide, with particularly profound consequences for children. In India, 75 percent of kids under age five suffer from iron deficiency, which impairs cognitive function; nearly half of all Indian children suffer stunted growth. Lack of good nutrition impedes brain development, educational outcomes, and job prospects, which affects the quality of life in communities, and, ultimately, a nation's economy. Researchers estimate that nutritional deficits can cut GDP by 12 percent globally. Childhood nutrition, then, is an obvious place for practical activists to focus their efforts, as its ripples have enormous long-range impact.

After many years of fits and starts to confront the problem, we are finally beginning to see a solution at scale, and every undercurrent discussed in this book played a part.

This story begins in 1985, with a father-and-son team of inventors. James and Duffy Cox, of Bellingham, Washington, wondered if they could create extra value from broken rice grains by grinding them into flour and then mixing that flour with nutrients like iron and folic acid. Flour, milk, and salt have been fortified with vitamins and minerals in the United States since the early 1940s. But boosting the nutritional value of basic food staples is much newer in the developing world. The Coxes, wondering if they could devise a product to address this lack, extruded their enriched rice flour through a pasta machine to create rice kernels supercharged with nutrients. But now what? How to incorporate their super-rice into the diets of malnourished people around the world?

It was a fantastic idea, simple and seemingly straightforward. But as we saw with Vaccine Vial Monitors in Chapter 6, simple solutions do not necessarily mean an easy fix. Making a rice pasta that smelled, tasted, and looked like regular rice when cooked—even when packed with calcium, zinc, folic acid, thiamin, and iron—took the Coxes more than 10 years. Marketing it to the world, however, meant navigating the same maze of technical and regulatory obstacles that confront anyone trying to scale a good idea, so in 1997 the Coxes turned over their patent to PATH.

Even for a large organization with vast international experience like PATH, the complexities of bringing fortified rice to the world were daunting. For one thing, people in different countries eat different types of rice, so we needed to tailor the product individually for each. The weight of these super-kernels was also critical—how to distribute the pasta evenly within a sack of rice so that it wouldn't sift to the bottom? Answering that question took 11 years of testing and refinement—including the invention of a special milling machine—but by 2008, PATH had perfected a process whereby one grain of fortified pasta could be blended with regular rice during production. When cooked, each fortified grain dissolved, infusing the whole pot with nutrients.

So far, so good. But the fortified rice still had to be approved by regulators—was it a food or a medicine? Each category had specific stipulations, and getting PATH's simple product through that maze took years, necessitating partnerships with a range of global institutions, including the Department of Biotechnology in India, the Ministry of Agriculture in Brazil, the Federal University of Vicosa in Brazil, the University of Toronto, and others.

Ultra Rice, as we came to call it, was more expensive to make, which was yet another problem since it was targeted at the poor. Further, families in the world's most destitute regions don't buy rice in boxes at the grocery story. They scoop it out of bulk bins at a farmer's market. So how could this high-nutrient product find its way into the food chain? We are still negotiating that hurdle to this day.

But the governments of India, Myanmar, and Brazil—having risen from the bottom of the economic pyramid to the low-mid section of our stubby economic diamond—have begun to buy Ultra Rice for distribution to school feeding programs. In India, that means dispatching a fleet of 79 trucks to 28 schools across 72 miles every day, all of them arriving in time for the 1 p.m. lunch hour. In the east Indian state of Odisha, the United Nations World Food Program is bringing Ultra Rice to 98,000 children. Another 450,000 kids in 2,600 schools across the southwestern state of Karnataka eat it daily.

In Myanmar, the government recently began serving Ultra Rice at orphanages, as well as schools. Young factory workers in Yangon, gathering at the Sunday Café program described in Chapter 4, are taught about the importance of child nutrition and encouraged to serve Ultra Rice to their families. (Clinical trials have found a significant increase in iron among kids who eat the product.) And within two years of introducing Ultra Rice in Brazil, it had reached 2.5 million customers, most of them middle and low income.

While this amazing story is still unfolding, it exemplifies many of the undercurrents I've described in this book. Countries with strengthening economies have moved from the bottom to the middle of the diamond, allowing them to purchase and adapt Ultra Rice to suit their people. This, in turn, creates new business lines for local millers who are answering community demands about the product's taste and convenience. Concern about access for the poor is pushing activists toward finding new ways of reaching the most vulnerable women and children—an equity focus, if ever there was. Digital tools, particularly around public education through social media and surveillance of uptake, track the manufacture, distribution, and nutritional effects of Ultra Rice. Of course, the entire journey is a textbook example of the partnerships and adaptations required to bring any solution to scale. The only thing that bothers me about this story is how long it took, and how many kids around the world still aren't getting this desperately needed intervention.

Like every example in this book, Ultra Rice shows that turning a concept into action is eminently doable—even if it takes years and years. The most essential requirement is showing up. You must put your shoulder to the wheel and do the work, not simply lob complaints from the sidelines. But I was not always so clear on that. In my early days as a lawyer in Seattle, I got a sharp comeuppance on this point, delivered by a man who was impossible to ignore.

Bill Gates, Sr., father of the Microsoft co-founder, was a named partner at the law firm where I worked, and he was passionate about the venerable nonprofit organization United Way of King County. At a brownbag lunch that everyone in the office was pushed to attend, Gates talked about the group and its importance to our region. I was only a few years into my job at the firm, still raw from my experiences in refugee resettlement and gay activism, and I had my own ideas about the United Way. To me, it was in 1990 a risk-averse, out-of-date organization that seemed to ignore the needs of many new or historically marginalized communities (like immigrants and LGBTQI people) and often used bullying tactics to raise money.

"With all due respect," I stammered, raising my hand, "I think the United Way could do a better job including the whole community."

Several colleagues gave me a swift kick under the table. That was it, they told me later. I'd made a major, career-limiting blunder.

A few days later, Bill Sr. ambled into my office. He's a big guy, dignified and somewhat intimidating in his bearing. He had never visited me before. Here we go, I thought, I'm about to be canned.

But that's not what happened. Bill noted my strong opinions, asked what had prompted them, and listened thoughtfully as I talked about my experience working on the ground with marginalized groups. Finally, he suggested that I put my energy where my mouth was—in other words, channel my energy for outrage and criticism into action.

It was some of the most valuable advice of my career: there's nothing wrong with disagreeing. But if you do, be willing to engage. Show up. Try to be a bridge between the old and the new, rather than taking potshots. All these lessons are essential for practical activism.

Bill meant what he said. Within a few weeks, he'd asked me to sit down with the co-founder of Costco and several other business and civic leaders to help lead a strategic overhaul of our local United Way. I did, and later found myself chairing the board of a significantly redesigned organization. Some of that was due to being in the right place at the right time, or putting my wrong foot in the right mouth. But it also serves as a constant reminder to use whatever privileges we might have to jump in to address problems, rather than merely complain.

I've told that story many times to would-be activists. But today's problems are so enormous, they sometimes say. Where do I even begin to make a dent? I often hear this from students, friends, and associates in the corporate world. All of them are intelligent, empathic folks, outraged at injustice. All of them are searching for ways to get involved. Even professional activists struggle, at times, to find a path forward.

But you don't have to have a degree in public health or policy to contribute to meaningful social change. You don't even have to work for a community nonprofit or international agency. If my work has taught me anything, it's that there are practical activists channeling undercurrents to make a difference within every sector of our society, and often in places you might not expect.

I've profiled a few of them here in hopes that readers see aspects of themselves reflected in the ways these people found a means to turn their own outrage into optimism for driving change.

As I mentioned in the Introduction, Michael was a student in my social innovation class at Stanford's business school. He usually sat in the back, lobbing questions about the metrics used to measure success in global development. I'd interpreted this as skepticism about the whole endeavor, so I was pleasantly surprised when Michael emailed me in the summer of 2019, long after the class had ended, asking to talk.

I'd always seen him as a hard worker—Michael had already built a career as an investment analyst at Bain Capital—and I could hear his smarts. But I'd misunderstood where his incisive questions were coming from. They weren't designed to undercut. Rather, Michael was searching. He was a dyed-in-the-wool capitalist but convinced that the profit-above-all corporate model was unsustainable, and he wanted to figure out a new role for business in society. His particular interest was shareholder activism—in short, ways that investors can use their collective power as owners to force corporations to do good. Typically, shareholders are seen as having only one interest: profit. But in Michael's view this is not necessarily true. Nor does he think shareholder influence need be a bad thing. He believed its power could be channeled to push positive social change.

And, as it happened, he was working on a book about that.

"So, tell me about the book project," I said, once we'd caught up.

"It's called *Accountable: The Rise of Citizen Capitalism*, and basically, it says that by holding corporations accountable to a deeper purpose, we can make capitalism into something both prosperous and good. What do you think?"

"That's the trillion-dollar question. I mean, look at all the noise about that from politicians."

"But I'm not talking about politics—at least not yet," said Michael, who ended up working on several presidential campaigns. "I'm thinking about this as a businessperson. What I mean is, do you think 'stakeholder capitalism' can actually change things?"

"Yes and no," I told him. "In an economy that's booming for the elites, no one with power has much of an incentive to make big changes. But it's true that there's a new conversation happening, partly driven by people like you, and I think it will be increasingly difficult for business leaders not to have a position related to social impact."

"But isn't that just greenwashing?" asked my ever-skeptical mentee, referring to the much-derided habit of corporations making superficial—though highly visible—gestures toward environmentally oriented side projects. "Do you think it will ever go deeper?"

I had thought a lot about this question over the years, and I was happy to have a moment outside of class to talk it through with someone I'd come to view as part of the next generation of practical activists. Michael was interested in broad systems change, particularly around the inclusion of marginalized groups, neighborhood revitalization, and environmental sustainability. He was not looking for feel-good, Band-Aid approaches. And he grasped the concept of the value chain, the fundamental importance of scaling. Most of all, he was riveted on the metrics by which companies hold themselves accountable.

"I do think so, yes, but only when social-impact metrics—clear, measurable results—become part of everyday financial reporting requirements," I said. "Proxies for profit, in other words. Not just a page in the annual report. The kind of corporate activism you're talking about will only take root when it's measured as part of a business's operating metrics for evaluating success."

"Exactly!" said Michael, unable to hide his enthusiasm.

I smiled into the phone. Will we ever see this happen? There's a long road ahead, but more companies are moving in that direction. In 2020, the Bank of America committed to incorporate outcomes around social good in its annual self-evaluation. Many countries in Asia now require corporate social responsibility programs and mandate that a certain percentage of pre-tax dollars go toward them. It's a nascent movement but spreading.

I can't help but be encouraged when talking with the new generation of global citizens like Michael. An activist in the most pragmatic sense, he cares deeply about the future of this planet and figuring out how the corporate world fits into that equation. He's also a young man after my own heart. Michael is not satisfied by researching a problem, or even publishing books about it. He wants to see action. Real change.

I pointed him toward companies like Unilever, Tata, and Econet, each of which is reshaping itself along these lines and could well impact business trends through this century. I suggested that he think about emerging business opportunities as more countries move from their old base-of-the-pyramid status into the widening middle of the global-economy diamond. I told him about my own efforts to change the way large multinationals work with stakeholders, and that reminded me of Celine Soubranne.

A Frenchwoman, Celine began her career as a journalist at *Le Figaro*. Today she is the chief corporate responsibility officer at AXA Group, one of the oldest and largest insurance and financial services firms in the world. A lot of business leaders talk about social responsibility and, as I've just noted, a few are reshaping their corporate strategies to reflect this. But AXA's top officers have fully embraced the belief that slowing climate change, promoting human health, and advancing inclusion will ultimately benefit their company's bottom line. For an insurer, fewer climate-based disasters and less serious illness mean smaller payouts and more profit, to put it plainly. That leads to greater resiliency and increased agility for addressing new customer demands. Celine has been a major driver behind that realization at AXA.

In 2019, during a conversation with UNESCO's Assistant Director-General for Natural Sciences, she explicitly spoke to the link between biodiversity and corporate interests. "It is often forgotten that behind the tragedy of the disappearance of an animal or plant species, there is also a human victim. From an insurer's point of view, this is an alarming observation," she pointed out. "A forest helps regulate a region's water cycle, which improves flood resilience and mitigates the adverse effects of heat waves. Biodiversity also enables the efficient functioning of agriculture and human nutrition. In fact, biodiversity is essential for health."

Pursuit of a strategy to support environmental sustainability has not come without a cost, however. In 2019, AXA announced that it was pulling all investment from the tobacco industry and, by 2040, would do the same for coal. Simultaneously, the corporation launched a new investment product, Transition Bonds, which finances energy transition projects to encourage low-carbon technologies. AXA also anticipates doubling its investment in green technologies from 12 billion Euros in 2020 to 24 billion by 2023.

Fourteen years ago, when she started in Communications at the insurance giant, Celine envisioned none of this. She'd wanted a career that promoted the common good, and she struggled to reconcile that goal with work at a major multinational corporation. The efficacy of private enterprise, however, impressed her.

Might there be a way to use that corporate strength for promoting a healthier world?

Sustainability was not seen as much of a career path when Celine announced to her colleagues at AXA that she intended to become director of that department. "Are you crazy?" they asked. "Are you sure?"

She was indeed. Celine believes in changing the world by changing corporate culture. "It is a kind of activism," she says. "My job is to provide the social insight, and to link the projects of our various departments—procurement, finance, insurance, HR—with the state of the world."

Celine's impact is obvious beyond investment strategies. Since she took the helm as chief corporate responsibility officer in 2018, AXA has stopped covering nonsustainable forestry operations and fishing vessels that refuse to declare their catch volumes to authorities.

Many of the undercurrents discussed in this book play out through her work, particularly in AXA's emphasis on providing financial products to marginalized groups and using data analytics for better risk management.

But if I had to name one thing that qualifies Celine as a practical activist, I'd point to her passion for bridge building. It's what makes her leap out of bed every morning, a drive to connect the agendas of business and social innovation. "It's gone way beyond a question of image," she says. "AXA now sees sustainability as relevant to profitability."

Working on world change from a completely different vantage point is Myo Myint Aung. A physician who studied in the United States on a Fulbright scholarship, Myo could have gone anywhere after graduate school. He's bright, ambitious, personable, and well traveled. But Myanmar, his native country, is in the early stages of rebuilding itself as a democracy after a half-century of debilitating military rule, and Myo sees this transition as an opportunity.

What if he could help transform Myanmar's health system as the new government emerged—particularly as it related to the poor, who comprise about 25 percent of Myanmar's population? For a young man who had seen close up the power of strong digital and health systems in the United States, the possibilities were inspiring. In 2015, he returned home to raise his family in the capital city of Yangon, and soon became PATH's country director there.

Initially, Myo focused on nutrition. He helped get fortified Ultra Rice into community feeding programs so that children could advance from surviving to thriving. In Myanmar, many children receive only four years of schooling and, until recently, the government invested less than 1 percent of its GDP into its health and education systems. But Myo, the son of a physician who often accepted payment in bananas when patients had no money, has never become discouraged about the depth of need in Southeast Asia's poorest country. To the contrary, it seems to fire his drive. Increasingly, Myo has broadened his focus to include reproductive rights and education for adolescent girls, recognizing that elevating the status of women is one of the most effective ways to improve conditions for all people.

When not on the road, Myo occasionally meets with Myanmar's Minister of Health to discuss next-generation models for patient data as the country builds its new public health system. He is very much a professional activist, but also something of a social entrepreneur—practical and idealistic at once.

"What's the biggest opportunity for impact here?" I asked Myo as we traveled by cab through the jam-packed streets of Yangon in 2019. I often had such conversations with PATH's country directors, pushing them to think more ambitiously about bringing innovation to broken or nascent government systems.

"Digital, digital, digital," he said. "Yes, we have huge health challenges—our stats on maternal mortality, tuberculosis, and child nutrition are terrible. But we could make so much headway if we just had the data."

"Isn't that sort of the tail wagging the dog?" I said, playing devil's advocate. "A bunch of numbers and data points aren't going to fix an underresourced health system."

"No, of course not. But we have this unique moment. In Myanmar, we're rebuilding a lot of parts at the same time. If we could start with a better platform for managing patient information and understanding health trends, we would make better decisions. It could help us leapfrog ahead."

"So, what do you need?"

"It starts with policy. Getting the right technology will matter, but right now it's not about the newest mobile device—we've got plenty of cell towers. What we really need is a comprehensive strategy, a framework to ensure that we're doing this right, so that when we get the data, we're using it well."

"Myanmar and almost every country in the world," I sighed.

Myo was so right. We're still more focused on technological tools and gadgets than on the communities for whom we want them to work, or the systems that need to be rebuilt. We're still imposing digital solutions from afar, rather than providing the technical assistance countries are asking for.

Myanmar, however, is a fascinating case of a long-isolated country transitioning before our eyes into a twenty-first-century society. There is still political uncertainty, government corruption, and enormous poverty, yet also growing economic activity and evidence of inspiring social innovation. Poverty rates have dropped by half since 2005, and Myo puts women into positions of authority wherever he can, recognizing the power in equity. When I visited him at PATH's country office, his nearly all-female team was analyzing data, advising on community health needs, and generating ideas for new initiatives.

Remember Blessing Omakwu, the young Nigerian-American lawyer advocating for gender equality? Like Myo, she is a professional activist. But Blessing's journey toward this work was not driven only by her sense of outrage on matters of gender equity. Raised by deeply devout parents who founded a church and served as its pastors, Blessing struggled for years to reconcile her twin passions—gender equality and religious faith.

It helped her to realize that Jesus was an activist. But once Blessing satisfied herself that there was no conflict between her faith and self-image as a "gender-equality evangelist," she confronted a new challenge: the tendency within global development to ignore religious communities. In Nigeria, large multinational nonprofits may come and go. Government actors routinely fail. Religious groups pick up the slack. "Where do you go if you need help? Not to a government agency," Blessing says. "In Nigeria, the people teaching and providing food—it's faith-based organizations. Mosques and churches have been the ones founding and supporting schools and hospitals. If we don't bring religious actors into the conversation, I really believe we're wasting our time."

These tensions—between faith, gender equality, and the conventions of global development itself—present questions with which Blessing wrestles every day. At one point, she wondered if she could even call herself an activist. She was a lawyer but never envisioned litigating. She was an evangelist for women in power but never got much satisfaction from marching in the streets. Blessing sees herself as an activist closer to the model I've described in this book, someone who promotes social change through policy work, bridge-building, and shifting mindsets, one person at a time.

"I believe in the importance of laws and policies as important goalposts on the journey to social change. But I know conversations and changed minds are the GPS that gets us there," Blessing says, though she has done her share of marching. In 2014, Blessing was part of a group of activists who successfully lobbied the Nigerian National Assembly to pass legislation on national healthcare. To my mind, she is exactly what we need more of, someone who ties together street activism with behind-the-scenes bridge-building and an orientation toward policy.

But Blessing brings it all back to the personal, to one-on-one relationships. "Conversations can transform minds, which can transform cultures, which can transform nations," she likes to say.

Where Myo and Blessing have made careers in activism, and Michael and Celine are pushing social change from within corporate structures, there are important roles for people who see themselves as just regular folks. These are my neighbors, and yours, individuals like my friend Heather, a busy mom with school-aged kids and an aging parent to care for.

Heather is high-energy and opinionated, but also full of worry about the future of our country and planet. She believes that community involvement is the answer. But she has very little time to devote, and I think she spends too much of it fanning the flames of her outrage by watching Stephen Colbert.

Heather cares about the arts, education, and giving minority students more access to opportunity. We've discussed the undercurrents in this book and how they are reshaping our world. After some soul-searching, Heather decided that her way of pitching in would be through supporting children's theater. Is that practical activism? Absolutely. Heather joined the board of a group that brings professional theater to young audiences, often in low-income schools, where there is a plethora of evidence that it helps improve student engagement. The satisfaction of that work encouraged her to push further, bringing similar programming to juvenile detention halls.

This is community-centered work, for sure (the theater group goes nowhere unless invited). It is fighting for equity by bringing arts education to families that have not had enough access to it and, increasingly, it uses digital platforms to live-stream performances.

One of the most interesting aspects of Heather's activism is the way it spans several areas of focus simultaneously (the arts, education, and juvenile justice). I sense this hunger for broad impact among lots of new activists. And it makes perfect sense.

Another colleague of mine, Katherine, specifically wanted to find a way of marrying work on climate change—which she considers *the* major issue of our time—with health, where she had spent most of her career. Katherine thought there might be a nexus between nutrition innovations, such as new, nonanimal proteins, and the problem of respiratory illness in smoggy cities strangled by carbon dioxide. She discussed these kinds of health-and-environment crossovers every chance she got—in schools, with friends, and through her professional circles—and eventually one of those conversations involved me. Katherine was looking for a way to take action beyond adjusting her personal carbon footprint. Something with visible impact.

Around the same time, I was having a beer with the head of The Nature Conservancy, and I mentioned this lack of crossover between the global health and climate movements. (The two often view each other as competitors for both political mindshare and funding.) In 2016, these various conversations birthed the Bridge Collaborative, a nonprofit dedicated to driving bigger change, faster, through cross-sector work.

Data was a natural place to start, since activists working on both climate change and public health have tons of information, though they rarely share it. (Malaria control is a perfect example: researchers in Zambia have reams of meteorological data that they use to predict mosquito population spikes and likely disease hotspots. No doubt, climate change scientists could make use of it too.) The Bridge Collaborative is not yet generating anything close to the attention Greta Thurnberg commands. But it has connected with more than 150 collaborators from dozens of organizations around the world, created a playbook for shaping cross-sector policies, and built a framework for thinking about the ways different areas of activism might bolster one another. It also exemplifies a grassroots effort that could eventually scale up and help save the planet.

Often, people who reach a certain level of professional success say they want to "give back" or "pay it forward." But none of the people I've just introduced are wealthy, and each is poised to make a real difference. They aren't waiting to become rich or famous before engaging as activists. I am, of course, deeply appreciative of the generous billionaires who've committed their resources and time to addressing social problems. But there is an implicit message in the notion of "giving back," a suggestion that it's okay to "take" until we're rich enough, or closing in on retirement. It implies that civic activism is something that can wait until we're "ready," or that leadership around social change should be directed by the wealthy. All of these are ideas I reject.

At the 2014 Skoll Forum, a global conference on social entrepreneurship and activism hosted in the university town of Oxford, England, former eBay president Jeff Skoll spoke at the opening event with Richard Branson, CEO of Virgin Group. Two of the wealthiest men in the world, both said they'd thought little about social impact or community involvement while building their careers. I'll admit it, I cringed at the message this sent to their student audience and the young activists also listening. Inarguably, each has made significant contributions, but I don't think this is how practical activism usually works.

Most social change is undertaken by busy people with limited time, money, and capacity. Most activists never get rich or start foundations. Most will not be leading high-profile global initiatives. Practical activism starts, very often, with kitchen table conversations about an outrage at a social problem and an idea to address it, a small notion that can grow big. It's built by galvanizing communities to join the fight. It's hard, gritty work that takes an immense amount of perseverance. Most of its heroes are unsung.

Of course, you need money, strategy, and leadership to turn beliefs into reality. You need talent and partnerships and some sort of value proposition that demonstrates the benefit of a product or service. This book is not a how-to manual for achieving those goals. What I've offered is a discussion aimed at helping activists—professional, emergent, or aspiring—recognize some of the forces beneath the surface that are driving change and, most importantly, to prove that there are reasons for optimism in the midst of our outrage.

So, don't wave off the extra half-hour of conversation with a new friend or colleague. It might unleash a wellspring of energy to keep going. Whether with community champions in the cafes of Lubumbashi or Harlem, young technologists in Senegal or Vietnam, or political influencers in Geneva and Beijing, this is where I've found the encouragement to push past the inevitable challenges. These conversations are where we remind each other of the things that *are* working, in order to jump in and address the things that aren't. We point out the enormous power in social undercurrents. Then we get up from the table, march out the door, and turn our outrage into activism to change the world.

8

Catching Your Current

All of Us Can Change the World

Everybody can be great … because anybody can serve. You don't have to have a college degree to serve. You don't have to make your subject and verb agree to serve. You only need a heart full of grace. A soul generated by love.
                                                                    —*Martin Luther King Jr.*

EVEN THOUGH I had been engaged with global and national health security issues for many years—helping teams respond to Ebola epidemics in the Democratic Republic of the Congo, setting up Emergency Operations Centers in Vietnam and Senegal, sitting on panels and national congressional commissions on health security, and being an early participant in the founding of the Coalition for Epidemic Preparedness and Innovations (CEPI)—in March 2020 the novel coronavirus brought home the deeply human meaning behind all these discussions with an immediacy I had not seen before.

Rather than advising the WHO or Congress on strategies to address an outbreak, I found myself counseling my own son about whether he should go to work with a face mask, and helping friends weigh decisions about halting travel or closing their businesses due to a virus. Even as it has torn through communities, the COVID-19 pandemic has provided a visceral reminder of how truly interconnected our world is, effectively obliterating borderlines between local and global activism.

The complex scientific and economic issues that spooled out from the pandemic are beyond the scope of this book. Yet they underscore so many of the messages in *Undercurrents*: the ways terrifying daily headlines can dominate our thinking, even though long-range trendlines show that humans are, overall, getting healthier. In the midst of our fear—and in some cases outright panic—COVID-19 has also provided a clarifying sense of outrage. How is it possible that our world—and particularly my own country—can have so much wealth, technology, and know-how, yet be unprepared to counter such a foreseeable, disruptive threat to our health and economy? What does it say about our priorities when we consistently underfund health security programs, then stumble through the same boom-and-bust cycle with every outbreak? Why do we continuously allow the most vulnerable among us to inequitably bear the brunt of these crises? As the popular expression goes, "if you're not outraged, you're not paying attention."

The call to action in this book could not be more timely. With our societal fissures so starkly exposed, this is precisely the moment to channel all that outrage into meaningful, practical action. Terrifying as the first months of the COVID-19 pandemic were, when I stepped back to catch my breath I could not help being inspired anew by epidemiologists working tirelessly to understand the trajectory of the virus. I was dazzled by the data tools and algorithms inventors were creating to help scientists devise an intelligent response to the disease. At a scale never seen before, policymakers were looking to local communities for guidance on how to address business closures, employee well-being, health system management, and travel. Pharmaceutical companies and drug regulators demonstrated a willingness to accelerate new candidates for medicine and vaccines along the typically winding journey to scale. Small and medium-sized businesses jumped in to boost the supply chain for protective equipment, while multinational corporations demonstrated unprecedented readiness to offer their know-how and global reach in forging solutions. Most heartening of all, public health leaders—including at the federal level—spoke with unusual candor about the brutally inequitable toll that COVID-19, and all such crises, level on the poor. From those conversations we saw new protocols developed for the homeless, infirm, and our communities' most defenseless citizens. Full consequences of the pandemic may not be understood for years. But the immediate response has illuminated every undercurrent in this book, and its unlikely warriors—scientists, physicians, policymakers, and community leaders—have become the heroic practical activists of our time.

Whether you are fighting against an ancient disease like malaria or emergent pathogens like the novel coronavirus; addressing age-old discrimination between genders or facing down new challenges like cybersecurity; sitting in Lagos thinking about community safety hazards; or living in Shanghai worried about global threats to food security, activists of every kind will need to use every tool we've got to keep improving our world.

This book has been my effort to explain some of the ways such changemakers across our global community are tackling problems, and why those on the sidelines should be emboldened to step up and engage. It has been shaped by my experiences and observations over four decades. I've identified five macrotrends and undercurrents: the shift of demographics from our traditional pyramid to an emerging diamond model, the concept of communities as customers, the need to level the playing field to improve equity for all people, the positive power of digital disruption, and the surprisingly sexy middle, where we can adapt and scale innovation for greater impact.

But I have also attempted to look beyond my own trench to explore other disciplines and sectors. Certainly, there are more macrotrends and undercurrents, and within each, there are elements that overlap with others. But these are the forces I see as most promising for our collective future. They guide my thinking and give me hope.

While my greatest wish is that they do the same for you, what really matters is your own view of the future. Each of us has an opportunity to shape it—no matter how outraged (or content), activated (or complacent), experienced (or naïve) we may be. As I talk with people around the globe, I am often perplexed when they suggest that my work is important and theirs, by implication, is less so—as if my job somehow defines my ability to be an activist. Nothing could be further from the truth. As COVID-19 has made clear, you don't need to have a nonprofit job, be a wealthy philanthropist, or work as a frontline volunteer to approach life through the lens of activism. Almost all jobs have social value, and every person possesses the ability to affect their community. Whether you're a seasoned volunteer, a civic leader needing a boost, exploring a career transition, or just starting out as a beginner, there is opportunity all around us—every day—to bend the arc of our own stories toward progress for the world community. The work ahead is to find those undercurrents that resonate for you, individually, and use them to power your activism. Those opportunities will show up at different times and in different forms for every person reading these words. But, inevitably, the undercurrents I have described will shape our lives.

Finding purpose is an elusive but potent idea. I don't know if it's the answer to a fulfilling life. But I do believe that working to make the world a little bit better, every day, has a powerful, cumulative effect. For the practical activist in each of us, nothing is quite as satisfying as getting stuff done—stuff that matters. Some of us will launch lifesaving products. Or celebrate with devastated communities that have found the pulse of new life. Some will cheer once-struggling students as they cross a graduation stage, while others take quiet pride in watching a well-irrigated field blossom and flourish. Each of these moments creates the energy we need to keep pushing forward.

What I've just described is the kind of optimism that underpins all activism. And it brings to mind one last story. On a mid-October day in 2019, I stood under a makeshift tent in the blistering heat of western Kenya, handing out car keys and computers. The vehicles and machinery were muddy and used, but the feeling of accomplishment among the group of 30 invited guests was palpable. This region of Africa has one of the highest rates of HIV infection in the world, affecting an estimated 1.6 million people in 2018 and leaving more than 660,000 children orphaned by AIDS. Yet the scene outside Kakamega's Ministry of Health was joyful.

For two decades, PATH had been working in Kenya to help the community prevent and treat this devastating disease, and we had now reached a milestone. Mortality rates in Kakamega had been cut by more than half during the prior eight years, and almost all children born to HIV-positive mothers were receiving treatment to prevent transmission of the disease. PATH had helped train more than 2,000 Kenyan health workers to provide family planning services and maternity care. We had, in fact, been so successful that there was no longer any role for us. Kakamega had the resources—both technical and financial—to develop its own solutions, so PATH was closing up shop. Which is why I was there, handing over the keys.

"A bittersweet moment," I said to the county minister of health as we sat together, waiting for the ceremony to begin.

She nodded. "I feel the same way."

I knew what was coming next.

"Even though we are sad you're leaving, we need to be able to do this ourselves, and now we can."

The accomplishments in Kakamega were due not only to the skills of a deeply dedicated staff. They had been powered by the steady movement of Kenya's citizens from poverty into the middle class. Political reform, economic development, and innovative health and education programs had supercharged investment in the country and more than quintupled Kenya's GDP in 15 years. New spending had cut child mortality rates and brought nearly all children into primary school. Literacy rates had climbed to 80 percent.

Still, this was a day of mixed emotions. Winding up our work meant terminating employment for more than 40 Kenyans (though most had already been rehired by local organizations). Some of the staff felt that they'd done years of heavy lifting only to be rewarded by having the rug pulled out from under them. Yet in so many ways, this was development at its best.

"Guys, this is what we're set up to do," I said. "This is why we're here—to be the bridge between no capability and local groups flying on their own."

I handed the keys to the minister of health, who climbed into one of the pickup trucks, started the engine, and headed down the road to continue her work of building a better world.

Appendix A: Notes and Further Reading

I HOPE THIS BOOK stimulates further exploration, research, and even activism. Here are a few expanded notes and references related to each chapter.

Introduction

It is fitting that this book starts in a UNCHR refugee camp, as immigration and refugee issues remain to this day one of the most outrageous issues of our times, in desperate need of activism and innovation. For more insights, check out UNHCR, the UN Refugee Agency (www.unhcr.org) and the International Rescue Committee (www.rescue.org). Further analysis of refugee resettlement and immigration policies and criteria can be found at the U.S. Committee for Refugees and Immigrants (www.refugees.org). Two (of many) great books describing the refugee experience are Dave Eggers's *What Is the What* (2014), and Dina Nayeri's *The Ungrateful Refugee* (2019).

My appointment at the Stanford Graduate School of Business is on the faculty of its Center for Social Innovation (www.gsb .stanford.edu/faculty-research/centers-initiatives/csi). There are many excellent journals and books on the emerging field of social innovation, among them, *The Stanford Social Innovation Review* (www.ssir.org), *Innovation and Scaling for Impact: How Effective Social Enterprises Do It* (by Christian Seelos and Johanna Mair, 2017), and *Social Innovation: How Societies Find the Power to Change* (Geoff Morgan, 2019). And the inaugural quote comes from one of my favorite autobiographies, by a hero for my generation, Nelson Mandela's *Long Walk to Freedom* (1994).

Chapter 1: Reading the Waters

The gay rights movement over the past four decades has been documented by many. One of the most important books at the height of the AIDS epidemic was Randy Schilts's *And the Band Played On: Politics, People and the AIDS Epidemic* (1987). Other more current views on the LGBTQI activism and HIV include Lillian Faderman's *The Gay Revolution: The Story of a Struggle* (2015) and David France's *How to Survive a Plague: The Story of How Activists and Scientists Tamed AIDS* (2017). We are strong supporters of the extraordinary work of Lambda Legal (www.lambdalegal.org), a strong advocate for LGBTQI rights nationally, and OutRight (www.outrightinternational.org), which does the same globally. Scholarship and commentary on China's rise are endless. A few books of note include Philip P. Pan's *Out of Mao's Shadow: The Struggle for the Soul of New China* (2008), Peter Hessler's *Country Driving: A Journey Through China from Farm to Factory* (2011), and David Shambaugh's *China Reader: Rising Power* (2016). Corbis was started by Bill Gates in 1991, sold most of its assets over the past 10 years, and is now known as Branded Entertainment Network. Hundreds of articles covered its journey. See www.wikipedia .org/wiki/Branded_Entertainment_Network, "Leonardo on Disk:

Deal of the 16th Century" (Stephen Manes, *New York Times*, December 3, 1996); "A Century's Photo History Destined for Life in a Mine" (Sarah Boxer, *New York Times*, April 15, 2001); and "The Decade-Long Image Licensing War Is Suddenly Over" (*Time*, January 2, 2016). McKinsey & Company's social sector work (where I worked for five years) can be explored at www.mckinsey .com/industries/social-sector/how-we-help-clients, and my current work as co-chair of the World Health Organization's Digital Health Technical Advisory Group is described at www.who.int/health-topics/digital-health/dh-tag-membership.

The United Nations' Sustainable Development Goals (SDGs), shaping the global development agenda today, are summarized at www.sustainabledevelopment.un.org. The field of global health and development is vast, well covered, and endlessly studied, but some of the best ongoing sources are the *Devex International Development* media platform at www.devex.com and *The Guardian's* ongoing coverage at www.theguardian.com/global-development. Other terrific sources include the Center for Global Development (www .cgdev.org), the Center for Strategic and International Studies (www.csis.org/topics/global-health), and The Bill & Melinda Gates Foundation (www.gatesfoundation.org). PATH (www.path.org) has been around for over 40 years and has contributed greatly to global health innovations. It has been honored by many others, including the Hilton Foundation (www.hiltonfoundation.org/humanitarian-prize/laureates/path) and repeatedly by The Tech Museum (now Tech Interactive) (www.thetech.org/tech-awards-honors-top-international-innovators).

Chapter 2: Pyramid to Diamond

The demographic shifts in terms of poverty and wealth are studied by many. Perhaps the best source for country-level data is the World Bank and its annual indicators, found at www.datatopics.worldbank .org/world-development-indicators/the-world-by-income-and-region. Oxfam annually releases critical data and analyses of global inequality; see www.oxfam.org/en/tags/inequality. Others are studying these changing sociofinancial demographics at a more regional or local level, such as the International Monetary Fund (www.imf.org/external/np/fad/inequality), the Brookings Institution (www.brookings.edu/topic/income-inequality-social-mobility), and the UK Parliament (www.theguardian.com/business/2018/apr/07/global-inequality-tipping-point-2030). Many scholars have examined "bottom of the pyramid" economics, particularly C. K. Prahalad and Stuart L. Hart's *The Fortune at the Bottom of the Pyramid* (2004) and Paul Colliers's *The Bottom Billion* (2007). Important contributions to this issue can be found in the Nobel Prize–winning study *Poor Economics: A Radical Rethinking of the Way to Fight Global Poverty* (Abhijit Banerjee and Esther Duflo, 2011) and *Dead Aid: Why Aid Is Not Working and a Better Way for Africa* (Dambisa Moyo, 2009). The swelling middle class that is shaping our new diamond has been examined by many; see, for example, www.foreignpolicy.com/2012/05/16/the-global-middle-class-is-bigger-than-we-thought and https://www.brookings.edu/blog/future-development/2018/09/27/a-global-tipping-point-half-the-world-is-now-middle lwtype="spaced"-class-or-wealthier.

This chapter also focused on the HIV epidemic and LGBTQI community in Vietnam, which is described by UNAIDS (www.unaids.org/en/regionscountries/countries/vietnam) and featured by PBS (www.pbs.org/newshour/world/vietnam-learning-embrace-life-hiv). The PEPFAR program support of private sector partnerships like Glink is described at www.state.gov/public-private-partnerships-pepfar. Many studies and books focus on the private sector's engagement in social impact. For introductory ideas see Michael Porter and Mark Kramer's influential article in the February 2011 *Harvard Business Review* entitled "Creating Shared Value." More recent views on stakeholder capitalism and corporate social impact can be found in the World Economic Forum's "Davos Manifesto 2020" (www.weforum.org/agenda/2019/12/davos-manifesto-2020-the-universal-purpose-of-a-company-in-the-fourth-industrial-revolution), the U.S. Business Roundtable's revised "Statement on the Purpose of a Corporation" (www.businessroundtable.org/business-roundtable-redefines-the-purpose-of-a-corporation-to-promote-an-economy-that-serves-all-americans), and a growing number of revised regulatory frameworks for companies, such as the UK's Revised Regulatory Code (www.frc.org.uk/getattachment/88bd8c45-50ea-4841-95b0-d2f4f48069a2/2018-UK-Corporate-Governance-Code).

As we explore new forms of aid and development from other countries, much has been written about China's emerging development plans and its One Belt One Road Policy, for example in the Council on Foreign Relations' "China's Massive Belt and Road Initiative" (www.cfr.org/backgrounder/chinas-massive-belt-and-road-initiative). China's new International Aid and Development Agency can be better understood by reviewing the Carnegie Endowment's 2019 study, "Ins and Outs of China's International Development Agency," at www.carnegieendowment.org/2019/09/02/ins-and-outs-of-china-s-international-development-agency-pub-7973. In May 2019, Devex covered some of the recent conferences and conversations about the "decolonization of global health" (www.devex.com/news/the-activists-trying-to-decolonize-global-health-94904). The United Nations Development Program elaborates further on other tools and models to measure global development and well-being, such as the Gini Coefficient and Human Development Index, at http://hdr.undp.org/sites/default/files/hdrp_2010_35.pdf.

The Decade of Vaccines is described by WHO at www.who.int/immunization/global_vaccine_action_plan/DoV_GVAP_2012_2020/en while Gavi and its many successes are featured at www.gavi.org. PATH's partnership in expanding the China-made Japanese encephalitis vaccine across Asia is described at www.path.org/japanese-encephalitis and was covered by considerable media, including a February 15, 2013 *Washington Post* article at www.washingtonpost.com/wp-dyn/content/article/2006/07/

26/AR2006072600249. And the work of Challenge Seattle on its response to Covid-19 was described by Erika Fry's April 17, 2020 article in *Fortune*, "Saving a City: How Seattle's Corporate Giants Banded Together to Flatten the Curve" (www.fortune.com/longform/coronavirus-seattle-flatten-curve-amazon-microsoft-starbucks-nordstrom-costco-covid-19-outbreak/?swaswa).

Chapter 3: Communities Are the Customers

For further exploration of the global challenge to fight our most deadly infectious disease—tuberculosis—the global Stop TB Partnership (www.stoptb.org) is always a good resource. The Public Private Interface Agency partnership to control TB in India is more fully described at www.path.org/articles/finding-missing-millions-importance-private-sector-engagement-eliminating-tuberculosis/ and has been further covered in March 2020 by *The Better India* at www.thebetterindia.com/218614/how-to-treat-tuberculosis-care-treatment-diagnosis-cough-healthcare-india/.   Community-based activism is not a new concept but is finding more voice in global discussions. To learn more, look at *Walk Out Walk On: A Learning Journey into Communities Daring to Live the Future Now* by Margaret Wheatley and Deborah Frieze (2011) and *Gaining Ground: A Blueprint for Community-Based International Development* by Joan Velasquez (2014). A great case study is Tostan (www.tostan.org), an Africa-based organization working directly with rural communities that are leading their own development.

A range of perspectives are revealed when reviewing the many studies and analyses of the legacy of PEPFAR, from the Bipartisan Policy Center's 2015 "The Case for Strategic Health Diplomacy" (www.bipartisanpolicy.org/report/the-case-for-strategic-health-diplomacy-a-study-of-pepfar), to Devex's 2018 article "A Look at PEPFAR's Strategy: Controversies and Motivations" (www.devex.com/news/a-look-at-pepfar-s-strategy-controversies-and-motivations-93038), to the Council on Foreign Relations' 2018

brief "PEPFAR's Impact on Global Health Is Fading" (www.cfr
.org/expert-brief/pepfars-impact-global-health-fading). Similarly, a
range of assessments of what worked and didn't in the DRC Ebola
outbreak can be found in *Foreign Affairs* at www.cfr.org/in-brief/
escalating-ebola-crisis-drc or in *The New Humanitarian* at www
.thenewhumanitarian.org/opinion/2019/08/01/Ebola-outbreak-
community-response-Congo. For more information on the concept
and examples of human-centered design, explore the Institute
for Human Centered Design at www.humancentereddesign.org
and one of its many proponents in the social innovation field,
Ideo.org at www.ideo.org. WHO has promoted the concept of
"self-care" in global health (see www.who.int/reproductivehealth/
self-care-interventions) and scientists and activists are studying it more (see www.thelancet.com/journals/langlo/article/
PIIS2214-109X(20)30160-1/fulltext). One of the examples in this
chapter was PATH's uterine balloon tamponade, which is further
explained at www.path.org/articles/the-ubt-a-simple-device-to-
save-mothers-lives/. Community-based approaches to the U.S.
opioid crisis are gaining ground. Harvard's Howard Koh lays out
these opportunities in the September 19, 2017 JAMA *Forum* article
"Community-Based Prevention and Strategies for the Opioid
Crisis," and *The Missoulian* (www.missoulian.com) has extensively
covered the crisis in Montana. Efforts to address HIV in the DRC,
particularly among men who have sex with men and sex workers,
have continued for years. Use of community HIV champions, like
the Congolese men who gave me my copper bracelet, was reviewed
in the a 2015 *Journal of AIDS* article (www.semanticscholar.org/
paper/Applying-innovative-approaches-for-reaching-men-who-
Mulongo-Kapila/d5c65ef8429a0c2d8faf713660f5808985a7e673).

Chapter 4: Leveling the Field

Countless scholars and activists have been thinking and writing
about our ageless search for more equity and equality across many

dimensions. A couple of recent books on my bookshelf are Chimamanda Ngozi Adichie's *We Should All Be Feminists* (2015) and Michael Kaufman's *The Time Has Come: Why Men Must Join the Gender Equality Revolution*. I have been inspired by amazing women leaders. In addition to Blessing, Melinda, Mabel, Malala, Michelle, and Michele, who are mentioned in the book, I am hopeful that Michele Barry's efforts at Stanford, now called Women Leaders in Global Health (WomenLift Health: www.womenlifthealth .org), will advance another generation of women leaders in global health. Global Health 50/50 continues to provide further insight and benchmarks on this issue (https://globalhealth5050 .org/2020report/). To learn more about the global fight against cervical cancer, see the World Cancer Research Fund (www.wcrf .org/dietandcancer/cancer-trends/cervical-cancer-statistics); and for more about the HPV Vaccine, see Gavi (www.gavi.org/types-support/vaccine-support/human-papillomavirus). The extraordinary impact of girls' education on human development is detailed in *What Works in Girls' Education: Evidence for the World's Best Investment* (Gene Sperling and Rebecca Winthrop, 2015), and of course is more personally described in Malala Yousafzai's *I am Malala, the Girl Who Stood Up for Education and Was Shot by the Taliban* (2013). Blessing Okmakwu's *The She Tank* (www.theshetank) is a modern think tank dedicated to promoting gender equality and women's rights in Africa. Among the extensive reporting on the development sector's challenges during the #metoo movement, *The Guardian*'s Kate Hodal provided an overview on October 14, 2019, in "Aid Sector Forced into Greater Transparency by #MeToo Movement."

Hans Rosling is always a reliable source for understanding trends and facts associated with global health and development, and his book *Factfulness: Ten Reasons We're Wrong About the World—and Why Things Are Better Than You Think* (with Anna Rosling Ronnlund and Ola Rosling, 2018) is terrific. Steven Pinker's *Enlightenment Now: The Case for Reason, Science, Humanism, and*

Progress (2018) underscores some of these same themes. For more on the story of the Sayana Press, the self-injecting long-lasting contraceptive, see Katie Thomas's "Pfizer and Aid Groups Team Up on Contraceptives for the Developing World" (*New York Times*, November 13, 2014). For more on Robin Hammond's "Where Love Is Illegal" exhibit, see Masha Green's "The Photographer Documenting Anti-Gay Discrimination Across the World" (*New Yorker*, February 10, 2019). And for more on PEPFAR's DREAMS program that funded Mama Sisi's Safe Space in Kisumu, Kenya, see www.state.gov/pepfar-dreams-partnership/.

Chapter 5: Digital Disruption

The Global Health Security Agenda (www.ghsagenda.org) provides funding and support for setting up Emergency Operations Centers around the globe, including the one in the Democratic Republic of Congo (DRC). The DRC's Digital Agency was a landmark for that country and is featured at www.path.org/articles/digital-congo-ebola/. The digital response to COVID-19 illustrated a full range of digital health opportunities and challenges. See "Virtual Health Care in the Era of COVID-19" by Paul Webster (*The Lancet*, April 22, 2020), and the World Health Organization's overview at https://www.who.int/news-room/detail/03-04-2020-digital-technology-for-covid-19-response. For more details on the Better Immunization Data Initiative in Zambia and Tanzania, go to https://bidinitiative.org, and for more on Visualize No Malaria go to www.tableau.com/about/blog/2019/4/visualize-no-malaria-crosses-new-frontiers-fight-against-disease. Khan Academy (www.khanacademy.org) has been featured as an educational game-changer. The World Economic Forum has convened and sponsored many programs at the intersection of technology, health, and development as part of its Fourth Industrial Revolution framework. See www.weforum.org/agenda/2016/01/the-fourth-industrial-revolution-what-it-means-and-how-to-respond. Much has been written about Maria Ressa and her journalism career and activism in the Philippines. Among the best is Josh Hammer's "The Journalist vs. the President, with Life on the Line" (*New York Times*, October 15, 2019).

Chapter 6: The Surprisingly Sexy Middle

There are many wonderful programs encouraging, funding, and celebrating early-stage social innovators and social entrepreneurs, including the Bill & Melinda Gates Foundation's Grand Challenges (https://gcgh.grandchallenges.org), the Skoll Foundation Awards for Social Entrepreneurship (www.skoll.org/about/skoll-awards/), and the TED Audacious Project (https://audaciousproject.org), not to mention countless academic and research recognitions. The Bridgespan Group provides an overview of these models at "Unleashing Philanthropy's Big Bets for Social Change" (*Stanford Social Innovation Review*, Spring 2019). The MacArthur Foundation's 100&Change (www.macfound.org/programs/100change/strategy/) has become a beacon in big-bet end-to-end philanthropy.

The challenges of the vaccine cold chain and some of the emerging solutions are outlined by UNICEF at www.unicef .org/supply/what-cold-chain. The *Vaccine Vial Monitor* has been evaluated for many articles and studies; my own Stanford GSB case study, "Vaccine Vial Monitors: The Little Big Thing" can be found at www.gsb.stanford.edu/faculty-research/case-studies/ vaccine-vial-monitors-little-big-thing-taking-social-innovation-scale. "Pilotitis" has become a term of art in the development sector, and its impact on digital health is discussed at www.blog .praekeltfoundation.org/post/147639334452/curing-pilot-itis-for-mhealth. Efforts to shape, develop, and scale up responses to COVID-19 were numerous; perhaps one of the most important has been the WHO ACT Accelerator, the Gates Foundation and Wellcome Trust's COVID-19 Therapeutics Accelerator (www .gatesfoundation.org/TheOptimist/Articles/coronavirus-mark-suzman-therapeutics) and the WHO's Access to COVID-19 Tools

(ACT) Accelerator (www.who.int/who-documents-detail/access-to-covid-19-tools-(act)-accelerator). The Rockefeller Foundation (www.rockefellerfoundation.org) and the Tides Foundation (www.tides.org) have also contributed significantly to the field of scaling innovations and solutions.

Beyond his contributions with *The New Yorker's* "Slow Ideas" article referenced herein, Atul Gawande has been a remarkable health leader and journalist. Read more about him and his work at www.atulgawande.com. The issues of juvenile incarceration are profound in the United States. See Patrick McCarthy's "The Road to Scale Runs Through the Public Sector" (*Stanford Social Innovation Review*, Spring 2014). We are a strong supporter of local programs on these issues, like Choose180 (www.choose180.org). An account of the long fight for same-sex marriage in the United States can be found in *Love Wins: The Lovers and Lawyers Who Fought the Landmark Case for Marriage Equality* (Debbie Cenziper and Jim Obergefell, 2016). Representative Ted Yoho explains his own story of becoming an ardent supporter of foreign assistance in a December 25, 2016, *Ocala Star-Banner* opinion page (www.ocala.com/opinion/20161225/ted-yoho-new-economic-approach-to-foreign-aid). Keller Rinaudo's journey developing and scaling up Zipline (www.flyzipline.com) has been featured many times, including in *Fast Company's* "Zipline Mastered Medical Drone Delivery in Africa—Now It's Coming to the U.S." (Amy Fraley, March 10, 2020).

Chapter 7: The Undercurrents Ripple and Converge

The story of using Ultra Rice to combat global undernutrition can be further explored at www.path.org/articles/harnessing-power-fortified-rice-stronger-healthier-india/. Bill Gates Sr. served as a role model for many of us practical activists. I appreciated his own 2009 book, *Showing Up for Life: Thoughts on the Gifts of a Lifetime*. Michael O'Neill and Warren Valdmanis's new book *Accountable:*

Rise of Citizen Capitalism (2020) explores important issues of the role of business in society. Also explore the work my friend Paul Polman is doing to tap into "the power of a courageous collective unleashing business to achieve our Global Goals" at www.imagine .one. AXA has been a leader among the largest multinational corporations in the world in terms of integrating social impact into their products and business lines. I hope to see a case study developed on their impact, but in the meantime you can find out more at www.axa.com/en/about-us/corporate-responsibility-strategy. The role of social entrepreneurs in Myanmar, like Myo Myint Aung, have been described by Catherine Cheney in *Devex* ("The Rise of Myanmar's Social Entrepreneurs," December 7, 2017). I'm proud of the early work of the Bridge Collaborative of thinking about new models for collaborations across the field of global health and development and climate action, as further described at www .bridgecollaborativeglobal.org. And the annual Skoll World Forum (www.skoll.org/skoll-world-forum/) has contributed greatly to the conversations and energy around social entrepreneurship and innovation. I hope to see new practical activists there in the future.

Chapter 8: Catching Your Current

The Coalition for Epidemic Preparedness Innovations (CEPI) was a prescient move by the global community to be ready to take on new pathogens, even if COVID-19 came along early in CEPI's development journey. For more about CEPI and its fight to develop new vaccines, see www.cepi.net. Finally, I further describe handing off the keys to the county minister of health in western Kenya in my essay "Stepping Away, Looking Forward" posted on LinkedIn on January 4, 2020, my last day at PATH (www.linkedin.com/pulse/ stepping-away-looking-forward-steve-davis).

Appendix B: Organizations Mentioned in This Book

ACT-UP: www.actupny.org

Annie E. Casey Foundation: www.aecf.org

Better Immunization Data Initiative: www.bidinitiative.org

Bill & Melinda Gates Foundation: www.gatesfoundation.org

Bloomberg Philanthropies: www.bloomberg.org

Bridge Collaborative: www.bridgecollaborativeglobal.org

CARE: www.care-international.org

Challenge Seattle: www.challengeseattle.com

Coalition for Epidemic Preparedness Innovations (CEPI): www.cepi.net

Co-Impact: www.co-impact.org

Dangote Foundation: www.dangote.com/foundation

d.light: www.dlight.com

Digital Green: www.digitalgreen.org

Gavi, the Vaccine Alliance: www.gavi.org

Girls Not Brides: www.girlsnotbrides.org

Girls Opportunity Alliance: www.obama.org/girlsopportunityalliance

GiveDirectly: https://www.givedirectly.org

Global Fund to Fight AIDS, Tuberculosis and Malaria (Global Fund): www.theglobalfund.org

Global Health 50/50: www.globalhealth5050.org

Global Partnerships: www.globalpartnerships.org

Hilton Foundation: www.hiltonfoundation.org

Ideo.org: www.ideo.org

International Rescue Committee: www.rescue.org

Khan Academy: www.khanacademy.org

Lambda Legal: www.lambdalegal.org

Lambert House: www.lamberthouse.org

Landesa: www.landesa.org

MacArthur Foundation: www.macfound.org

Malala Fund: www.malala.org

Mercy Corps: www.mercycorps.org

MIT Media Labs: www.media.mit.edu

NPower: www.npower.org

One Acre Fund: www.oneacrefund.org

OutRight: www.outrightinternational.org

Oxfam: www.oxfam.org

PATH: www.path.org

Philanthropy University: www.philanthropyu.org

Pro Mujer: www.promujer.org

Rappler: www.rappler.com

Rotary clubs: www.rotary.org

Sesame Workshop: www.sesameworkshop.org

She Tank: www.theshetank.org

Skoll Foundation: www.skollfoundation.org

Stanford Center for Innovation in Global Health: www.global health.stanford.edu

Stanford Graduate School of Business Center for Social Innovation: www.gsb.stanford.edu/faculty-research/centers-initiatives/csi

Tata Trust: www.tatatrust.org

TED: www.ted.com

The Nature Conservancy: www.nature.org

United Nations Development Program (UNDP): www.en.undp.org

United Nations Education, Scientific and Cultural Organization (UNESCO): www.en.unesco.org

United Nations High Commission on Refugees (UNHCR): www.unhcr.org

United Nations International Children's Emergency Fund (UNICEF): www.unicef.org

United Nations World Food Programme (WFP): www.wfpusa.org

United States Agency for International Development (USAID): www.usaid.gov

U.S. Centers for Disease Control (CDC): www.cdc.gov

U.S. President's Emergency Plan for AIDS Relief (PEPFAR): www.pepafar.org

Visualize No Malaria: www.path.org/visualize-no-malaria

Wellcome Trust: www.wellcome.ac.uk

Women Deliver: www.womendeliver.org

World Bank Global Financing Facility for Women, Children and Adolescents (GFF): www.globalfinancingfacility.org

World Economic Forum: www.weforum.org

World Health Organization (WHO): www.who.int

Zipline: www.flyzipline.com

Acknowledgments

WRITING A BOOK is a journey. This one reflects friendships and lessons learned over a lifetime. Many people have helped usher me along that road.

The changemakers mentioned or profiled in *Undercurrents* remind me every day of the power in practical activism. For their insight, energy, patience, and grace, thanks go to Myo Myint Aung, Michele Barrie, Kim Green, Justin Hamilton, Joel Holsinger, Deborah Kristensen, Le Minh Thanh, Ousmane Ly, Alex Ng, Michael O'Leary, Blessing Omakwu, Maria Ressa, Keller Rinaudo, Lucy Sanday, Celine Soubranne, and Shibu Vijayan. It has been an honor and daily inspiration to see the world through your eyes. I would be remiss not to give a nod to the Lao soccer-playing refugee who sparked much of this work; I hope your dreams came true.

Beyond these colleagues and partners, many of them from PATH, my views have also been shaped by prior work with brilliant thinkers across the public, private, and social sectors. Several agreed to share their perspectives as I honed my ideas for this book. For their invaluable expertise, I thank Arnaud Bernaert at the World Economic Forum; Michael Conway at McKinsey & Company; Yinuo Li at the Bill & Melinda Gates Foundation;

185

Bernhard Schwartlander at the World Health Organization; and Ed Whiting at Wellcome Trust.

Additional thanks go to the many supporters of PATH and global health innovation. Three should be mentioned specifically: The Rockefeller Foundation and Fondation Botnar, which supported my work on the COVID-19 pandemic while I wrote this book. Many of the projects highlighted in it would not exist at all without backing from the Bill & Melinda Gates Foundation, a major partner in so much activism around the globe. I am grateful to the foundation and to Bill and Melinda personally, as longtime colleagues, mentors, and friends. I look forward to further collaborations.

Thanks as well to Brian Neill, Kelly Talbot, and the team at John Wiley & Sons for their support and astute editing. And to Susan Briggs, Lisa Cohen, Bob Evans, Greg Shaw, Carla Sandine, and Katie Smith Milway, who provided helpful feedback on the manuscript's balance, content, and tone. A special shout-out to Katie, who convinced me to take on this project and helped me get it going. And without Linda Ettinger and Shelby Clayton keeping me organized and on track, who knows where I'd be. Any errors or omissions, however, are all mine.

My journey as a practical activist has been continually shaped by the powerful example set by my parents, Martha and Carl Davis, in our beloved Montana. Their model of balancing family, community, and service has not always been easy to follow, but it inspires me every day. For their unwavering support of me and my complicated life, thank you to my entire extended family—biological and chosen.

My deep love and gratitude to my son, Ben, who teaches me what it means to keep growing and whose presence in my life is a reminder of the heart at the center of this work. Most of all, I want to thank Bob for just everything.

Steve Davis
Seattle, Washington
May 2020

Special Thanks

THIS BOOK would neither have been possible nor turned into a readable and coherent manuscript without the enormous contributions of journalist and author Claudia Rowe. Claudia has focused her 30-year career on writing about the ways public policy affects the lives of children and families. She is a winner of the Washington State Book Award, a Casey Medal for Meritorious Journalism, and numerous other national honors. I am deeply grateful to her for her creative and engaging determination in helping shape my ideas and experiences into a narrative of currents and stories. Whether wandering the streets of Yangon or Hanoi together, or sharing drafts over Covid-induced Zoom calls, our work together exemplifies productive partnerships. I am deeply grateful for our collaboration and friendship.

About the Author

Steve Davis is a lecturer at the Stanford Graduate School of Business. He serves as co-chair of the World Health Organization's Digital Health Technical Advisory Group and is a member of numerous boards and advisory committees. He is the former president and CEO of PATH, a leading global health innovation organization; former director of social innovation at McKinsey & Company, a global consultancy; and former CEO of Corbis, a digital media pioneer. With degrees from Princeton University, the University of Washington, and Columbia Law School, he speaks and writes regularly about the intersection of innovation, technology, and social impact. He lives with his family in Seattle, Washington.

Index

191